Wings of the Morning

Pauline Lewis

Pauline Lewis tells her story

J6D Publications

Published by:
J6D Publications
9 Parnell Close
Littlethorpe
Leicestershire
LE19 2JS

on behalf of:
Pauline Lewis
12 Hawkhurst Court
Porthcawl
CF36 3NU

ISBN: 0-9549500-2-X

CONTENTS

FOREWORD

My wife Desma and I first met Pauline Thompson as she flew into the Laiagam airstrip, almost 7,000 ft above sea level, in what was then known as the 'Territory of Papua and New Guinea.' There was a great contrast between this 'English rose' and the other missionaries who had been exposed to the sun's ultra violet rays in the highlands of this tropical land. Pauline seemed a lot more suited to the garden parties where English ladies would gather, sipping tea and enjoying cucumber sandwiches, than the primitive surrounds of missionary work in such a remote region of the other side of the world.

This book, 'Wings of the Morning' is the story of how wrong those first impressions were. This was a lady in the true sense of the word, but one who experienced the call of God upon her life. One who was prepared to adjust her life-style and adapt her teaching skills to reach the children of this 'land that time forgot.'

The story gives hope to every individual that hears the call of God. Pauline walks us through some of the intimate experiences that she had to face along the way, before she could know the full expression of God's purpose for her life. The physical restrictions and illnesses experienced would have caused many to give up on the dream, but not so with this woman of spiritual insight and resolute character.

The determination to learn the language of the people in both Papua New Guinea and Ghana where Pauline served, is a story in itself. Overcoming the fears of isolation and the accompanying loneliness, is a further demonstration of the commitment of the writer.

Having been the Field Superintendent when Pauline came to Papua New Guinea, as it is now known, it was greatly beneficial to have on staff such a lady, who was used in the manifestation of the Holy Spirit. Still today, I recall the word of prophecy when the Lord challenged the large missionary staff to enter into 'sheer abandonment to His will.'

The romantic ending of the story in this book keeps the reader wanting to skip to the next chapter. The constant willingness of Pauline to put 'God's will first', has been gloriously rewarded. The words of the Psalmist have come to reality. 'Delight yourself in the LORD and he will give you the desires of your heart.' (Psalm 37:4 NIV)

I am satisfied that there are many men and women serving the Lord today in far distant lands, who were little children being lovingly taught by Pauline Lewis during her effective years of exciting, adventurous, missionary service.

John W.J. Hewitt
Superintendent (1963-1969)
Apostolic Church Mission, Papua New Guinea
President (1980-1994)
Apostolic Church Australia

The Hewitt family as I knew them. Now they are all serving the Lord.

INTRODUCTION

The clouds had come down to cover the mountain and we huddled inside the little house made of sticks and grass. There was a fire of course in the centre of the room, for though we were in the tropics it could be very cold high up in the mountains as we were, but there was no chimney. That would make the house cold they told us. I tried to keep out of the smoke. I had made my embarrassing trip into the bushes to find some semblance of a toilet hole. It was Bank Holiday Saturday, and back in the village in Penygroes in South Wales all my friends were gathering in their very best clothes, hats, gloves and all, for the first service of the international convention. I laughed to myself and wondered what they would have thought if they could have seen me in all my disarray! My legs were tucked uncomfortably under me now as I listened to see how much I could understand of the conversation. I had been in the highlands for a few weeks, studying the language for an hour each day when I returned from the school where I taught in English. This was to be my chance to see how much I had learned. Alas, I had not understood one word. I noticed Akuni, one of the school boys who had carried my loads, assisted me through the bogs and would serve as my interpreter. Holding court, he was waving his arms in a circular movement. 'What are you telling them, Akuni?' I asked. 'I am telling them that you come from right underneath the world.'

Brought up in the United Kingdom, we had always thought that we were on top. It was Australia that was 'down under' but now I was learning differently. To each, his own home is the centre. So here was I, on top of the world, but feeling that I was at the uttermost part of the earth.

How had this happened? I was not adventurous by nature. I hadn't even crossed the Channel until I was well in my twenties, and I would rather have gone without a meal than go into a cafe on my own. I had been brought up in suburbia, definitely from a 'sheltered home,' as our Education lecturer used to tell us, and we were not even of an evangelical persuasion. I had no concern for 'the lost,' having been taught that God's purpose for their salvation was in an age to come.

Introduction

So how was it that I had come on my own to work with this mission, believing that we were obeying Jesus' commission to go into all the world and preach the gospel and make disciples of every creature? It is quite a story, and as I believe God has called me to write for his glory, I am recording as much as I can remember.

When I left London airport to set out to Papua New Guinea, a dear friend, May Evans, gave me a promise from the Bible which was a great comfort, 'even there shall thy hand lead me.' It is from this verse, in Psalm 139, that I have taken the title for this story, 'Wings of the Morning.'

My stomach is never too happy at being in the air, but nevertheless it is a thrill to look out beyond the wing tips and see a blanket of snow white cloud between you and the earth. In the highlands of Papua New Guinea we did not have to be airborne to be above the clouds. By evening time they had usually descended to drench us in their cold and darkness but we would awake to find the air clean and bracing and the clouds, fast being burned up by the sun, now drifting in cotton wool softness in the valleys below us. We felt we were on the wings of the morning.

CHAPTER ONE—BEGINNINGS

A baby lay in her pram, conscious of the sunshine dappling the curtains, and of her mother's voice, somewhere in the background, telling her sister, 'Don't you wake Pauline.' But Mary, older by just twenty months, was having a game of beep-bo with her. A grin spread over the baby's face, for she knew that she must not make a noise. It was a delicious secret between the two of them.

That is one of my earliest memories for I was that baby. Another is of a little stone grotto in the garden. There was a bench inside, but outside were niches in the stone. John, Mary and I were each sitting in one. I was supremely happy to be doing the same as my big brother and sister.

That was in the little three bedroom house in 29 Woodlands Avenue, South Wanstead, where I was born. We had a beautiful natural park at one end of the road, and at the other the Wanstead Flats, a large expanse of grassland. Both had at one time been part of the Epping Forest, and had been bequeathed by Queen Victoria as a place of recreation for the people of London. Nurse Heskith had been the midwife for each of us children. I remember my parents used to laugh at her call, 'Cup of tea,' though whether she was bringing one to my mother, or calling someone to make one for her, I was never sure.

I was the third child to arrive in this little house. Having a boy and a girl they had hoped for another boy. I was to have been Paul. They couldn't have been too disappointed for they didn't send me back, just added -ine to my name.

I was registered as Pauline Thompson, born the 19th January 1931. I am told that I was a bonny baby, but at the age of two I had whooping cough very badly and my health was always a concern to my mother after that.

We moved from there to 22, Dover Road, only two streets away but a larger house, in time for Joy to be born, so I could not have been much more than two when the incidents occurred that are so secure in my memory.

But I had better introduce my parents, for without them I would not be here to tell this story. My father was registered as Captain Hubert Thompson. His first name was a source of great embarrassment to him and he had it removed by deed poll when he came of age. It seems that his father had been reading a book about a Captain Hedley at the time and he named this child Captain and his brother Hedley. I wondered what kind of parent would have so little feeling for the child he was labelling.

I never met my grandparents on my father's side. He was brought up in Forest Gate, at the other side of the Flats. I remember he used to walk across to collect rent from a house he owned. Was this where he was brought up? But I never saw the house. I do remember him telling us that the Pankhursts of suffragette fame were their neighbours, and what gracious ladies they were.

My father must have had music lessons as a boy, for he played the piano very beautifully. I have memories of him playing Elgar's Songs Without Words. They were probably a musical family for Marguerite, one of our cousins, became a professional musician.

I gathered that they were Primitive Methodists, as was his youngest brother, our beloved Uncle Hedley. He used to have a boys class, and having no children of their own, they became family to him and our lovely Auntie Ruth. They always had some story to tell us of their boys when we went to visit. My favourite was of one who had been a doctor in the mission hospital in Ilesha. He returned to a home practice and his surgery was in the house.

'Mummy, where's Daddy?' asked the little boy. 'Daddy is in the surgery, making people better.' Then his older sister came in. 'Where's Daddy?' Her brother had his own version, 'Daddy's in the surgery, kissing ladies better.'

My grandfather must have been austere, for Daddy used to tell the story of how he and his older brother had been taken to visit their grandmother. 'Say goodnight and God bless you, Grandma dear,' he was told. The boy stubbornly refused until at last he burst out, 'I can't say goodnight and God bless you Grandma dear.'

My father was obsessively tidy, to his sorrow, as my mother was just the opposite, her untidiness a constant thorn in his side. I remember him telling me how hurt he had been when he had returned from the war to find his father had disposed of all his kid gloves and other treasured possessions as if he had not expected him to come back. Obviously Daddy had inherited his tidiness from him.

They must have been brought up to go to church for we heard at one time of some dispute with the minister and from then on my father had finished with the traditional churches. It seemed to us that he had been happy to embrace the teaching of the Bible Students because there was no talk of repentance in order to be baptised and become one of the brethren.

He had held it against his father that he had not permitted him to go on to grammar school although his teacher had pleaded for him. At fourteen he was sent to work as a clerk at the Gas Light and Coke Company where, apart from the years of the first world war,he continued as an accountant until he retired.

A gracious gentleman who was his senior took Hubert under his wing. He had a reading society in his home, and it was through him that my father learned to love the classics and became a voracious reader. He had two beautiful chairs that had come from this gentleman's home and it was in one of these that he used to sit in his old age.

Although he was not a Christian at the time, he had high moral principles and when the war came he did non combatant duty on board H.M.S. Egypt which had been turned into a hospital ship. He had a photo of it on the wall in his study. He was one of a group of intellectuals on the ship who became close friends. One, 'Tubby' Britain, went on to become a fellow of Jesus College, Cambridge, and John and Mary were proud to have been introduced to him.

Was it through a public lecture, 'Where are the dead?' that my father came in contact with the Bible Students? I must have been told. I know that at last he had found a teaching which satisfied his intellect, without expecting an experience of repentance, though many of the originals in this movement already knew the Lord as Saviour and had left their chapels believing that they had found further truth.

Hubert was slight of build. With crisp waving hair that he swept back from an intellectual brow with two hair brushes, you would always notice him in a crowd. He could be the life and soul of a party with his quick wit as well as deep thoughts and I'm sure he must have broken many a girls heart, for he was thirty six when he, together with another young man, set out to cycle the hundred miles or more to visit a small outreach in Lowestoft, which was in the home of my mother's parents.

Beginnings

How my grandfather Lewis became involved with the Bible Students I am not sure, but I don't think my mother had any previous experience of church. I know they had followed the teaching of Charles Taize Russell, but when Judge Rutherford had taken over, organising the Watch Tower movement they had withdrawn and called themselves, for the sake of identity, The Associated Bible Students. How interested my mother was in the meetings I don't know, until my father came on the scene that is. She certainly was after that.

I was recently loaned a Charles Lettes leather bound school girls diary which had been given to her by H.T. As I read through I felt I was carried back to that time, and could see the tall, athletic girl with her enthusiasm for hockey, tennis and swimming, gradually being more drawn to Hubert, and to the teaching too which he had already embraced. Her plans to go to college were put aside. She was to leave her large family and the joys of living by the sea to come to London and was soon settled with the responsibilities of four small children and a husband sixteen years older than her, who suffered very badly with his nerves. She was only twenty when she married, and twenty five when I arrived on the scene.

My parents, Hubert and Kathleen

CHAPTER TWO—LOWESTOFT

It wasn't until I married Joel that I was told that my great grandfather Lewis was also Welsh. I never knew him. Indeed I did not know my grandfather very well, though I remember that I loved to go into his study and ask to see his little brass monkeys who see, hear and speak no evil. I gather from my aunts that he was an austere man and they had a very Victorian upbringing. The younger ones rebelled against his teaching. It was only my mother, and Uncle Jim, the brother next to her, who believed as he did. But often people show a different side to their grandchildren and I loved to stay in 6, Pakefield Avenue, Lowestoft, the old family home.

When I had gone exploring and became entangled in a mouse trap, it was my grandpa who rescued me. They tried to still my screams by pointing out that he had been hurt far more than I had. He had a blackened thumb nail to prove it, and I have never forgotten how he suffered for my sake.

My mother was a Cockney by birth for she had been born within the sound of Bow Bells. Her grandmother, Gran Hayward, who I knew as one of the family at Lowestoft, had lived in Paddington, so I suppose she must have been born in her house, but she was brought up in Horsham before they moved to Lowestoft. She told us stories a horse and trap and of milk being ladled out of the churn in her childhood there.   Gran had been widowed with six young children to bring up. She ran an old fashioned boarding house and life must have been very hard for her but she had energy left for fun for my mother recalls her chasing her boys around the kitchen with a kipper.

She was in her eighties when I knew her. Wrapped in shawls, with her fine grey hair hardly covering her scalp, and her little metal-framed glasses, she would sit with her sewing, making garments for us, her great grandchildren. She was almost stone deaf, but if we whispered something because we did not want her to hear she would be sure to pick it up. However, there was a day when my father had arrived unexpectedly. Each one who came into her room announced the news, 'Hubert's come.' At last Daddy himself came in. 'Oh,' says Gran, in great surprise, 'Hubert's come.' It became a family joke.

Lowestoft

She had a large bath chair with a step which was just right for a three year old to sit on. Off we would go in style. There were so many of my mother's brothers and sisters, or their boy friends, to help to push, and we would set out for the beach. We had our own hut and it was a great gathering place for the clan. I had to get off the step when we came down the ramp and when it was time to go home then it was all shoulders to the wheel to push it up again.

I can still recall those golden days when we played happily with our bucket and spade, always a wooden one as the metal ones were considered dangerous, though we longed to have one. When the sea was rough I loved to stand on the steps and have the waves splash over me, but one day when the sea was calm and shallow and the sun filtered through it making sparkling patterns on the sand beneath, I wandered happily pulling my little wooden boat behind me.

The sun did not always shine, even in my childhood. Sometimes I would run shivering into the hut to be rubbed down and dressed and given a hot drink, amid the smell of salt and wet sand and methylated spirits which was used for the primus stove.

The sun may not always have shone but those pre war days were golden ones for me at my grandparents home. I don't know if I was ever there on my own, but I was made to feel as if I was the only one. I was my grandmother's sweetheart, and I had all these aunts and uncles who used to tease me and play with me and take me for donkey rides or on the wonderful motor boats with the rubber buffers there in Kensington Gardens. It was such fun to bump into someone else, or to hide away at the other side of the pond when the man called your number to come in.

Nesta, my youngest aunt, was only six years older than John and still at school, and my fondest memories are of her.

'I always loved you as a baby,' she told me once. 'You were such a lovely sulky little thing.' I had fat little cheeks and I think I have always been rather solemn.

Christmas was a wonderful time there in Pakefield Avenue. All the families would gather, having played hockey on the beach to make sure we had a good appetite. There would be some wonderful silver novelties in the Christmas pudding which would reappear each year, until the time when the thimble could not be found. Had someone swallowed it unknowing? After that there were only silver threepenny pieces slipped on the side of the plate.

14

We were not encouraged to believe in Father Christmas. My parents were very strict that we must always be told what was true, but we did hang up our stockings for all that, and I woke once in the night and was very excited. I was sure I could hear Father Christmas creeping up the stairs, and our stockings were always filled with nuts and tangerines and chocolate money. Our larger presents would be given us downstairs, and we knew whom to thank.

There was a large deal table in the kitchen which would be filled with scrubbing boards and reckitts blue on a Monday. I'm not sure which day was for baking, but it was a sight to behold, laden with pies and pastries. I do remember a shelf of saucepan lids. We loved to have these as cymbals in our band until my poor grandma would come and declare that she could stand no more. We didn't really understand why.

Now it was laden with food. After we had eaten we would gather in the front room and play party games. 'Family Coach' was a favourite, when someone told the story, and each time the person we represented was mentioned, we would jump up and turn round but when they said 'family coach' there would be a stampede as we all had to change seats. 'Priest of the Parish' was another one when there was a rushing around to find another seat, and I marvel that the older ones had energy to play after a meal, but we children were in our element, and they did it for our sakes I suppose.

One game was 'Poor Pussy.' Puss had to kneel and miaow at someone's lap and they had to stroke him and say 'Poor pussy' three times without laughing. No one could miaow like my father, and try as she would he could always make my mother laugh.

Lowestoft was a fishing port and on occasions we would be taken to the harbour to see the boats come in with their loads of silver, wriggling fish. That was a smell not easily forgotten. Auntie Joan's in laws were fishermen and when I was older I begged to be taken on a night's fishing, but fortunately for me they would not agree. There was the thrill of seeing a 'bridger' too, when the swing bridge that was in the middle of the town would be closed and swing around to let a boat through to sail up the river Waveney.

Mother used to tell us how she dreaded there being a bridger when she was on her way to school, for then she would be late, and they would not allow the bridge as an excuse.

But 'it came to pass,' as all things must, and time came when the family home was sold. I had so wanted my Gran to live to be a hundred, and thought she had let me down when she died at eighty five, but I expect she felt she had lived long enough. Bob the dog died about the same time. Dear Bob, one of the kitchen cupboards had been taken out to make a bed for him and he would lie there letting me stroke his sandy coat. I was just as upset about Bob dying as my Gran and if anyone was ill after that I was so afraid they were going to die too.

I believe my grandfather died of cancer as did my grandmother, but that was later, in our home at Dover Road. I went into the large front bedroom and was horrified to see Grandpa smoking. They assured me that it was a medicinal cigarette but it had been instilled in me that smoking was evil and I was not altogether convinced.

When my dear Grandma died it was as if I had lost part of myself. If ever I felt unjustly treated or misunderstood I was going to run away to Grandma. Of course I did not really mean it but it was such a comfort to know that she was there for me and that I was special to her. She was my rock of refuge, my safe haven. She made a great effort to come shopping with me because she had promised, although my mother told her she was not well enough. She bought some milk jugs for my mother and I hid them for her and produced them on Christmas day, after she had died.

'Shall I read the next chapter, Grandma?' She was in bed all the time now, and when I came in from school I loved to read to her. 'Anne of Green Gables' was my favourite book and so I was sure it must be hers too.

'Would you read to me from the Bible, dear?' and I had to turn for her to the Psalms. Now of course I understand how that only God's word could meet her need, but I couldn't at the time.

When I got to bed I would hide under the clothes and break my heart for I knew without being told that she would not get better.

Coming home from school one day, my mother asked me to go to Janice's house for tea. No need to tell me. Grandma was dead. I did not shed a tear. They had all been poured out. A chapter of my life was closed, but how rich I was for the love and security that I had received from my grandparents.

Strangely I don't remember any 'meetings' in the Lowestoft home, or any religious teaching, though I suppose there must have been some. Yet my little life was being shaped, prepared for the journey that I must take on 'the wings of the morning.'

CHAPTER THREE—DOVER ROAD

As I have said, we moved to our house in Dover Road when Joy was expected. You see, they never did get another boy. I don't remember finding a new baby in the house, though I do remember staying with an aunt at the other side of London and my mother coming to bring me home again. I had to sit at one side of the carriage on the tube train, and my mother was opposite. She gave me such a sweet smile. It is a precious memory, though it is sad that she so rarely was able to express the deep love that she had for each one of us.

We all loved our little sister. She was Joy by name and joy by nature. With softly waving golden hair we only had to pretend to cry to get her to do what we wanted. But this could not last. The time came when her gentle voice turned to a shout and no longer could we twist her round our fingers. Of course, she was seven, when we all lose our delightful baby ways, but I did not understand this and felt that I had been robbed.

John and Mary were often scrapping. It must have been hard for John, having been the only one, to have a charming little girl getting all the attention that had been his, and now he had three sisters to try to keep in order. I adored my older sister, but I was jealous of her too, so we had our squabbles. When I was four they called me Fourleen, but soon after that Mary was six and I thought that to be six was the answer to all my problems. Alas, when at last I reached that wonderful age Mary by now was eight, and nothing had changed; but all in all we had lots of fun.

Dover Road was a large family house. The houses were built too close together so that the kitchen and scullery, as we called them, were dark rooms and I am sure were the cause of much of my mother's depression when we were in our teens, but Mother was there and so that was where we gathered. Every now and then, exasperated, she would chase us out. We had folding chairs in the kitchen and would put them together to make a track and slide over and under them.

We three girls shared a large bedroom with a wonderful view over the gardens, and away across the Wanstead Flats to London. If we went up to the attic bedroom and stood on a chest under the skylight window they told us that we could see the tower that remained from the Crystal Palace. We had been taken up there to see the whole sky lit up when the terrible fire took place. It was from our bedroom window that we could look out on the Bowling Club, where the Bible Students used to have their meetings, (that comes in another chapter) and where I wrote my first attempt at poetry as I looked at the stars.

'Mummy, Mummy! Look! I've got spots on my tummy.' I couldn't understand why my mother seemed upset. I was delighted, as now I would be allowed to go into the big bedroom with the others.

There used to be a stain on our bedroom ceiling. John had been put with us too while we were in quarantine with chicken pox. We must have been getting better and needed entertaining. John threw up a cherry from his fruit salad to see if he could catch it in his mouth. The mark was there for many a year.

There was another time when I was in bed with mumps. I was driving my mother mad because I was complaining about a blue bottle that had trapped itself inside the window. I was terrified of spiders and of anything that buzzed.

Uncle Jim arrived. 'Go and get rid of that fly for Pauline,' she begged. Up the stairs he bounced. 'Where's this blooming fly?'

Voice from bed. 'Uncle Jim, will you kill that blooming fly.' Oh dear, I was not supposed to use such language. It became a family joke. Another one was the time Mary, teasing me, pretended to sit on a gramophone record that was mine. Alas, she broke it. I followed my mother round all day begging her to 'dick it up with dicky duff.' I must have thought they had super glue in those days.

Meal times were wonderful. We would play guessing games and have spelling bees, and of course tea time was always at five o'clock so that we could listen to Children's Hour, and dear Uncle Mac and David, Out with Romany and Toy Town and wonderful serial stories such as Swallows and Amazons. I get a wave of nostalgia when I hear a piece of music that was used as a signature tune, even though often I cannot recall what it introduced. The wireless, as we called it then, was an important part of our home life.

I used to think that there was a row of houses inside its case where all the people whose voices we heard lived.

I wasn't so keen on the news because by then I had finished my meal and wanted to get down and play, but we had to sit still because my parents didn't want to be interrupted. Perhaps that is why I was never any good at current affairs in school. It was an important topic in war time. Once I determined to do better, and on hearing the announcement that 'general fog' was expected I sat up and asked, 'Who's he? I haven't heard of him before.'

But my early years were in that wonderful time of peace and I was unaware of the storm clouds that were brewing over Europe. I hadn't yet started school when George V and Queen Mary had their Silver Jubilee. John and Mary came home with commemorative mugs, and I was taken to the other side of the park to wave to their majesties.

I remember my parents standing around the wireless and calling for hush as King Edward the VIII made his abdication speech. I was five years old. I realised that it was a very sad occasion, though looking back we know that we were blessed to have such a godly man as King George to take the throne, and we followed the news of our two princesses with great interest. My parents took us up to London to see them as the family drove in an open horse drawn carriage when the king and queen were going on a visit to Canada.

But back to my home life. We never played in the street. We had a garden with a swing, and a sand pit. I loved the swing, where I would sing to myself happily for hours. We had a conservatory, and could play there if it was wet, and then there was the front room, where the piano was. It was only heated on special occasions. At Christmas, when all my father's relatives would come, the fire was lit for two days before. But it was a place where we could go. We used the table for unending games of Monopoly, and we played table tennis too, though the bevelled, rounded edges made our game rather unpredictable.

I don't remember ever playing with dolls, except to make clothes for them. I learned to knit when I was quite young.

'Mummy, look!' 'Oh, my, you're getting on like a house on fire.' I was delighted by her praise. But Joy had a scottie dog night dress case and we loved this and used to beg to have it in bed with us for a while. I used to like to tell my sisters stories when we were all in bed, but I so wanted the words to sound beautiful and probably they were fast asleep before I got to the plot, if there was one.

My parents were all for a healthy life style. They used to take a magazine, Health for All, and we ate plenty of vegetarian food. In New Guinea, and again in Ghana, people used to remark on my lovely English complexion, but I think it is because of the salads Mother gave us every day.

They loved to be out in the open air and would take us for long walks through Epping and Hainault Forest. (I suppose we must have done part of the journey by bus, for it wasn't until the war that we all had bicycles) I loved the wide open spaces, but I was often trailing behind the others because my little legs were so tired and I would be told to 'come on.'

Before Sunday morning breakfast, Daddy would take us into the park at the end of our road. We loved to see the baby rabbits at play, and sometimes would catch a glimpse of the bushy tail of a red squirrel or the flash of a kingfisher. There was a heronry by the ornamental waters and we loved to see the silent fishers suddenly swooping down and coming up with a fish in their beak.

Many mornings my father would go to the lake to swim, along with other fitness fanatics, even in the depth of winter. Alas, all his efforts at keep fit did not help his nerves, and though there were so many happy moments there was always the fear of an outburst. Often for him it would be just a flash in the pan but my mother would be wounded and our confidence shaken.

We had a little 'farm' shop, a general stores, across the main Aldersbrook Road, now part of the A12. We had to cross with caution, even in those days. The farm had gone before my time but the shop was always called 'the farm.' There were horses still in the stables, but after the war these stables were turned into garages and they had a filling station there.

A five minutes walk along the main road brought us to 'The Avenue,' where we were often sent on errands. Dr. Watters had his surgery on one corner, and the post office, greengrocers, stationers and some other shops were on the other. The first time I began to be aware of prices, potatoes were a penny a pound! It was a terminus for the trams. That must have been a long time ago.

Mother used to push Joy in the pram, and with Mary and me in tow, would walk across the flats to visit some of our Bible Student aunts and uncles. If we were lucky we would meet the 'stop me and buy one' man and mother would buy us a penny ice lolly. We longed for a cornet, but that was twopence and a special treat. John was at school by now, our time yet to come.

I have a distinct memory of coming home from one of our long family walks. The leaves were already changing colourand making a carpet that we could scuffle through, but I was crying because my little legs were tired and as so often happened I was left behind.

'Don't cry,' my mother told me as she came to take me by the hand. 'You're going to school tomorrow and school girls don't cry.'

I believed her, and hastily sniffed away my tears, even though Baby Soggy, as I thought he was called, was dragged screaming into the classroom for many a day. I later learned that his name was David. I was four and a half when I entered that awesome establishment that was going to devour the next fourteen years of my life, and do much to prepare me for this journey 'on the wings of the morning.'

Four little Thompsons: Pauline, Mary, Joy and John

CHAPTER FOUR—SCHOOL DAYS

'There you are, go and sit beside Pauline Mercer. She's from your street.'

I had no idea of who Pauline Mercer was and toddled hopelessly into the mass of little bodies seated on the wooden floor, eventually deciding to plonk myself down anywhere. An exasperated hand pulled me to my feet and placed me in the right class.

Fortunately we did not stay in that overwhelming assembly hall. The Infants were taken to their own building, but there were enough troubles there for me to cope with. There is one thing that prepared me for my future as a teacher and that was realising the importance of children wanting to come to school, for it wasn't until I reached the sixth form in the Grammar that I had ever thought there might be any pleasure in it.

Further along the main road was the Aldersbrook Homes, a terrible institution, as far as I was concerned, for children in the care of the council. They had no parents who would come and complain if they were unfairly punished, and though I am sure they were difficult to handle, the way they were treated made my life a misery too.

I have never forgotten seeing a little lad tied with laces into a chair and left crying piteously as we all filed out to play. When I was in the Juniors, the girl sitting next to me had combed her hair in class. I'm sure the comb was a prized possession, but the headmaster was offended by her action and sent her to the desk. She returned with her little hand bruised and swollen from the cruel strokes of the cane. This cloud of injustice hung over my school days.

In this first class we had to write on horrible squeaky chalk boards. The chalk would be given out, some pieces no bigger than a thumb nail, but one day the boy sharing my desk had a new half a stick. Just for fun I changed his with mine, but he hadn't even noticed.

'Look, I've got your piece,' I laughed. Alas, the teacher heard. There was a horrible silence as she walked round the room saying 'Isn't she a naughty girl,' while the children chimed, 'Yes Miss Chatterly.' I wanted to sink through the floor.

We heard later that she was to be married. We could not imagine that anyone would have wanted to marry her, but probably for her it was a way of escape.

My next teacher was Miss New, and we all adored her. I thought that was her name because she was new. Strangely I met her some years later and she was still Miss New, and still unmarried. Men did not have much discernment as far as I was concerned. She tried in vain to teach me to read. I remember having to sound out endless phonic charts, but though I could say c-a-t- I could not see any connection with the word cat. I'm not sure when the miracle happened, but I know that in the next class I was one of the best readers. One day I read the newspaper to our next door neighbours, Mrs Hooker and her step daughter, Norah, who were like family to us. They were most impressed. When I was teaching and some children seemed so 'thick' as far as reading was concerned, I had faith to believe that the miracle could happen for them too.

I had a lovely teacher in the Juniors and have memories of winning an Easter Egg in a china cup for my good hand writing. Then there was country dancing. I excelled at that, and netball. I was the shooter, and being smaller
than most of the other girls, could duck under their arms. Once I had the ball I was a sure shot.

But hanging as a cloud over any happiness was my fear of Mr. Lindley, the head master, and his dread swish of the cane. I only once was made to stand at the desk, unjustly at that, for I was much too scared to be naughty, and he sent me back to my room with a caution, but the fact that he was kind to me - I was a Thompson and one of his favourites,- could not erase from my mind his cruelty to the other children.

By now I was seven. It was 1938 and though I was not aware of it, other clouds were looming over our nation. In 1939 war was declared, but before I tell of what I remember of these years I think I should relate something of my earliest knowledge of God, for 'Wings of the morning' is most of all a spiritual journey.

As I have said, I have no recollection of any teaching about God in my grandparent's home. I don't remember my parents telling us about the Bible either, or teaching us to pray, except on Christmas morning. We had to listen to the story from the Bible and a prayer before we began to open our presents.

My father often read aloud to us. There were classics such as The Swiss Family Robinson, but on one occasion he read 'From Prison to Paradise,' the story of some martyrs of the reformation. My mother was not at all happy for she was very sensitive. Her mother used to faint at the mention of blood or anything horrible, and she used to say that she wished she could too because then people would stop. I have inherited this trait of being oversensitive to suffering, and try to make sure that I do not dwell on the dark side of life.

On a Sunday we could hear the solemn slow singing of hymns coming from the Bowling Club. We were not taken to the meetings until we were old enough to sit still. My mother had a helper who lived with us, our dear Auntie Warnes, a lovely plump Norfolk lady who was also of their persuasion. We loved her, but I know when the war came and people no longer had maids, my mother was glad enough to have her home to herself.

She and my parents would take turns to stay at home with us little ones. In this way we thought of going to the meetings as something greatly to be desired. There were so many 'aunties' and 'uncles' who made a fuss of us, and once we could read there was great turning of the pages to find the verse, and if we were very lucky we would be given an opportunity to read when it was a Bible Study.

They were always 'meetings' rather than services, and had a chairman and a speaker, or else open Bible study. When we heard our parents mention the chairman, we were convinced that they were talking about Cyril, the caretaker at the Baptist chapel, who pushed a load of chairs to and fro.

I was brought up to believe that we were very special. We had 'The Truth.' Lying in bed one night I wondered whether it was true about God and Jesus, or whether perhaps we were all part of a dream and that we were really ants or something.

I was a great reader and on one occasion we were on holiday and I had no story book. My mother gave me her Bible. Whether it was her suggestion I don't know, but I ended up reading the book of Job because it was a story. I don't think I ever got to the 'Happily ever after bit.' I often wonder how I did not know about the Gospels and the wonderful stories that are there.

I wasn't taught to say my prayers before going to sleep but there was one occasion when I prayed most earnestly. We had handwork once a week and were learning to weave. My pathetic piece of weaving seemed to be getting thinner and thinner and I was desperately worried about it. I used to stand with dread as we lined up to go into the craft room. But now I had prayed, so it was sure to be alright.

I couldn't believe it when I found my weaving looked just the same. God had let me down. I was never going to pray again.

Looking back I know that from then on it had ceased to shrink and I had ended up with a respectable strip of woven cloth that I had made into a little purse. God had answered my prayer, but not as I had expected and I held it against him.

Although we weren't told the gospel message in our meetings, I must have heard it as a child for it was while we were on a family holiday at Perranporth that we went to the Children's Special Service Mission meetings.

We stayed on a farm with a Mr. and Mrs. Spraggs and their children, Annie and Wenty. It was a long walk to the sea. We turned down past the shop with the Reckitts blue advertisement, where we could buy sweets, to take a foot path to the beach. Mother loaded up Joy's push chair with our swim suits, macs and towels and of course food for the day and we would trudge up the golden sands past the day trippers who all gathered up the near end until we came to the caves which made a wonderful shelter, although I don't remember it raining.

It was a fearsome place for little children because of the great Atlantic breakers, wonderful for surfers, but we had to content ourselves with splashing about in the rock pools. Once Joy was almost swept out to sea by a breaker and Mother upped with her skirt and rushed to her rescue. It was as exciting to us that Mother has shown her knickers as that Joy was saved from drowning.

Dad, always adventuresome, would take us climbing up the cliff paths which were terrifying to me, as were the mine shafts where we would drop stones down to see how many seconds we could count before we heard them fall below.

But we loved the children's meetings. I have often wondered how different my life would have been if I had known the simple gospel message, but I must certainly have heard it then.

We were seated on mats around the missioner who had made a boat out of sand, with flags and all. Standing in it, he was teaching us the chorus, 'Do you want a pilot? Signal then to Jesus. Do you want a pilot? Bid him come on board,' but I didn't understand the need for me to make a response, or the possibility of a personal relationship with the Saviour.

My father was enthusiastic about these services and bought us the Bible reading notes and the chorus books. Alas, our reading was soon forgotten, but the choruses became part of our lives. We used to stand around the piano while Daddy played. I remember the beautiful melody of 'Trust in the Lord with all your heart.' These scriptures in song were surely preparing us for the future. I still love to sing from the CSSM books.

We had two wonderful holidays at Perranporth, but the storm which had been gathering over Europe now broke. A chapter in my life had ended. Britain was at war.

CHAPTER FIVE—WAR YEARS

I always remember the month war was declared. It was September 1939. Joy had her birthday on the 15th. She was six. 'Come here,' John commanded and held her up by her heels. 'Now you are nine.'

We had gone on holiday to Littlehampton. Every year I would be so excited at the thought of a holiday and feared that it would never come. It was wonderful to be by the sea, though I was disappointed with the pebbly beach, not nearly as good as Lowestoft's soft sand. Little did I realise how nearly we didn't go that year, for everyone had their ears glued to the radio.

Bible Student friends living in Oxford had offered to take us in an emergency. My father now decided that we should not return to London but go straight there, but it was a cross country journey.

'Oxford? Why, I'm going there. I could take you.'

'But you don't understand. I have four children. And then there's our luggage.' They must have felt it a wonderful provision when this gentleman, living near Oxford, was able to bundle us all into his taxi.

We arrived on the Saturday night at Beaumont Buildings, to be welcomed with some surprise by a bleary eyed Mr. and Mrs Plummer, for Dad's telegram had not yet arrived. It was Sunday morning, the 3rd of September, that we heard the dread announcement, 'This country is now at war with Germany.'

Oxford was a solemn, awe inspiring city, with its ivy clad universities and martyrs memorials. We have happy memories of playing in the beautiful university parks for it was a golden Autumn and the time for conkers. Then there
was the 'humpity bridge' as we called it, over the Cherwell. We gave my mother a fright on one occasion when some soldiers befriended us and gave us a lift home in their car. We were solemnly warned never to do such a thing again.

It must have been awful for my mother, cooped up in two rooms with no outlook but brick walls, worrying about my father on his own in London and coping with the black out. It was while we were there that we were issued with gas masks and an identity card. I can still tell you my number, for we were made to memorise it. DXCV1636. Our numbers were in sequence, but my father's was different because he was in London. I was very proud when I had a leatherette case for my gas mask instead of just a cardboard box. We should be thankful that we never had to use them. Indeed that Autumn we wondered whether there really was a war. We did have a few weeks at school in Oxford. We were put in with other evacuees who had come with their teachers. They took us to the library and the teacher told me I was getting books that were too hard for me, but when she found I could read them she called me out to tell stories to the class. We were knitting woolly vests as handwork, but I am thankful mine was never finished. It would have been terribly itchy.

We only stayed a month or two for my mother was desperately ill with quinsies and the doctor told my father that there were worse things than bombs and to get her back in her own home.

John and Mary were then evacuated with their school. I am so thankful that I did not have that trauma, even though I was in London throughout those terrible years of the blitz for it was not until we had returned to London that the war, as far as we were concerned, really started.

Rationing did not start all at once. First it was one thing and then another. Mother registered two of us as vegetarian, and in that way we had a good supply of cheese to supplement our meagre meat ration. She was good at making what she called concoctions, which stood me in good stead on the mission field, when you had to cook with whatever came to hand.

The very first day milk was rationed Mother had used a new jug. Alas, John decided to see where it was made and spilt the whole pint.

We learned to make do with powdered eggs, and dried bananas, and to put grated carrots into the Christmas pudding.

'Mum, look! Look! Bananas.' There they were, hanging up in the fruiterers on Ilford Broadway. I couldn't understand why my mother told me not to be silly. I had not realised they were artificial.

We were allowed to use our own sweet ration, and this was a great joy to me. I only had fourpence a week. Our pocket money went up a halfpenny each year, but I always managed to save some, and to make my sweets last, to Mary's chagrin.

'Mrs. Thompson, Mrs. Thompson, may we come in?' We children sat up in our bunk beds to see our next door neighbours emerging from beneath the work bench on which our parents slept. We had spent each night in the cellar ever since the bombing had started, whether the warning had sounded or not. Joy's bed was on the bench at my parents feet and there were three bunks for John, Mary, and me on the bottom. We often used to sleep through the raids, for there were four ack ack guns at the end of our road that made a great noise, and so we were not too aware when bombs were falling. The doodle bombs had filled all of our hearts with fear as we heard the thin whine and then the silence that foretold a tragedy. But this night there had been a tremendous explosion, something different again.

Our house was semi detached, and bricks had been pulled out from the dividing wall so that if one of our houses should fall we might have a way of escape. It became a useful extra entrance, and our neighbours would often come and spend an evening with my parents playing cribbage. But now it was the middle of the night. We children often laughed at how comical Mrs. Hooker had looked, minus her teeth and with her hair in curlers.

Although we were living in the East End of London, a prime target for Hitler's bombing escapades, we children had a wonderfully protected existence. There were air raid shelters built by the school and we did spend an hour there. I still remember the smell of damp and concrete, and I didn't mind missing lessons because I had a book to read. But after that we who lived close by were allowed to hurry home, and we would run into the cellar only when we heard the planes overhead.

The night of the very first air raid we had cycled to visit some Bible Student friends who lived out in the country. We had to stay the night in their little Anderson shelter listening to the heavy drone of bombers flying overhead on their way to London.

The next morning we were out walking in a field, and ran for cover under the trees as we heard planes. They were flying low and we saw the dread black cross on the wings, as the German bombers were returning from their raid.

There was another occasion when I was very aware of the approach of the enemy. Staying with Uncle Jim and Auntie Edna and our little cousin Judy in Lowestoft, (was that after our school had been bombed?) we girls had been swimming and the siren sounded as we were dressing. We didn't have the sense to pick up our clothes and run for shelter as we were. Suddenly we were alone on the beach and flying straight toward us were these enemy planes.

We had noticed a convoy of ships leaving the port earlier. Now, as I stood petrified, trying to wriggle into clothes that seemed to have a mind of their own, I saw these ships stretched out as a line of defence. The pilots must have realised that they were coming within range of their guns, for now they turned in retreat.

There were many tragedies, even in our neighbourhood, during the war, but our parents did their best to shield us from the knowledge of them. Auntie Ruth and Uncle Hedley lived in Woodlands Avenue, and I was allowed to visit her on a Saturday morning, helping? her with her housework. I made sure that I ate all my greens if I stayed for dinner. 'I like Auntie Ruth's greens,' I told my mother. We were shocked when we went to see that pile of rubble that had been their house, but so thankful that they had not been in it. They moved away then to Southend. They had had enough of London.

My father was in the city when the docks were bombed and much of London ablaze, and had to try to make his way home through the devastation, and back again to work the next morning for life had to go on.

We had no gas for six weeks after they bombed the gas works. My mother coped by using the little warming oven that was over her coke boiler in the kitchen, cooking for herself and for many of the neighbours too. We used to have gas for everything, fridge, iron, water heater, because of Dad's work. I hated the iron as the flames used to lick up around your hand, but what a wonderful day it was when we had a gas poker to help to light the coal fires, and eventually one with a built in gas jet.

We had a cousin, Rupert, who was killed when the mine sweeper he was on was blown up. I remembered him as being tall and handsome, and thought it very sad, but we had not known him very well. It seemed remote from us children but I don't think his parents ever recovered from the tragedy.

Don, my mother's younger brother, was stationed at Woolwich at one time and used to come to us when he had leave. We children were delighted, but he sometimes found us a bit much to cope with.

Then one day he brought Audrey home. We thought there was no one so lovely as Audrey, and we still think so. The wedding must have been after the war because Don wore his 'demob' suit, but there were still so many restrictions it couldn't be a white wedding but she was a beautiful bride.

Then Nesta, our youngest aunt brought home a dashing naval officer to whom she had just become engaged. Our Mum, so much older, was mother to them all since Grandma had died. We thought it all very exciting, and really had no idea of the terrible dangers they were in, or how unpredictable was life.

The Bible Students, as did so many Christians, believed they could claim the protection of Psalm 91, and that they were abiding under the shadow of the Almighty, and indeed I don't think any of them suffered more than broken windows. My father once was walking home across the Flats when the warnings sounded. There was nowhere he could run for cover so he continued walking, but he was in terrible danger of being hit by shrapnel from the shells that were being fired. We often found pieces of horrible twisted metal in the garden.

There was one occasion when I heard my mother relating the effects of a bomb blast. 'A stone must have come in through the front window and landed in our wardrobe in the back.'

I went scarlet, for it was I who had put the stone there for some reason to hide it from Joy. I was much too embarrassed to tell my mother, and it would have been a pity to spoil her story, but I felt guilty about that for years.

The Bible Students were pacifists. It set us apart when we were at school because we wouldn't buy national saving bonds, and for the older ones there was the dread tribunal, though instead of being sent to prison as in the first war, most of them went happily to work on the land. At one time John's friend Derrick was working in some glass houses as part of his war effort, and we had happy cycle rides out to a farm where some of our 'uncles' were labourers. John was too young, but he had to face ostracism at school because he wouldn't join the cadets.

There were cows grazing on the Wanstead Flats now, and they would sometimes stray down our street and into our front garden for our iron railings and gates had long gone for the war effort. I remember our class going into Wanstead Park to gather acorns and hips to feed the pigs.

Then there was the allotment. They had dug up part of the Flats for this. We used to go as a family to work our patch and when the time came to bring home the harvest Joy's old pram was loaded up with carrots, beetroot and potatoes and we all helped to push it home.

We didn't envy John his task of following the tradesmen's horse drawn carts, so that he could collect manure for the allotment, but I think Dad made it worth his while.

Joy had not long learned to read when she asked, 'What's allummy-num, Mummy?' It was aluminium of course. They were asking for any pots and pans that could be used for aircraft construction.

We went to a demonstration of how to deal with incendiary bombs too, and Dad had to do his stint at fire watching. One Saturday Mary and I stayed at one of the big office blocks in the centre of London with Mother's friend, Phyl Vaughan as she was on fire watching duty. We could see right over London from the roof of the building.

Then there were the barrage balloons that floated high over our heads when the warnings sounded. We thought it a joke when we were told they were there to hold the cables up, but of course it was true.

One day there was an electrical storm. We watched in awe as one balloon after another was struck by lightning and disappeared in a mighty crackle and flash. John was rushing from the front to the back of the house exclaiming 'Oh boy! Oh boy! Oh boy!'

Four years had passed. We had become experts at make do and mend, for we couldn't get much with our clothes coupons and what we could was of poor quality. We made underwear from parachute silk, and our coats were made from old ones of our aunts and grandmother. Shoes were a great problem; my mother could never afford the coupons to get me shoes that fitted. I blame my painful feet now on those years of deprivation.

Was there ever to be an end to this terrible war? Then there was a steady roar of army lorries passing the end of our street on their way to the docks. There was a bump in the road and each one made its presence known as it passed with a mighty wallop. Nobody knew what, but we guessed that something was afoot and eventually we heard of the miracle of the D day landings.

One day I came into the large, sunny front bedroom at Dover Road and Mother told me that the war was over. We used to hear the church of St. Mary's chime from the other side of the park, but now the bells were ringing. I think it was because Mary was ill in bed that we had gathered there, but all I remember was the wonderful feeling of relief.

The terrible atomic bomb and VJ day soon followed and there were street parties to celebrate. They put up marquees on the Flats, and these ladies that I didn't know welcomed me so warmly. Maybe they recognised me as one of the Thompson clan, but probably they greeted each one of us as special, having survived this terrible war.

But there were other battles in my life, and happenings that were just as important to me as war in Europe, and they were all preparing me for the journey that I must take.

CHAPTER SIX—FRIENDS

I didn't make any lasting friendships at school. Being in the Bible Students we were different and so didn't fit in well. I used to try to hide behind the edge of the cupboard in school assembly so that no one would see that I was not singing 'Holy, holy, holy.' I love the hymn now, but at that time, 'God in three persons,' did not fit in with our theology.

'Do you believe in the Trinity?' I asked Janice, ready for once to seek to convince her of my beliefs, but her answer took the wind out of my sails.

'I'm not sure. I either do or I don't.' What could you say to that?

Mr. Lindley, my much feared head master, with his greasy trousers, his cigarette butts and his love of the cane, would often get in a jibe about the Bible Students, and if I was caught with my thoughts wandering, would suggest that I was 'lost in wonder, love and praise.' It would be many a year before I knew that such an experience was possible. We were not encouraged to bring our friends home from school. I'm sure my mother thought there were enough of us already. On one occasion Betty, who was brought up by an elderly aunt, begged me to ask if she could come to tea. I eventually yielded to her persuasion, but she never got an answer. I was made to stand in the corner, so I don't know how long poor Betty waited by the gate.

I have a feeling that it was this same Betty who instigated the teasing of some of the other girls. There was Jean who must have had some glandular trouble and was fat and rather slow. If bated sufficiently she would provide entertainment by swearing.

I begged Betty to leave her alone. 'Suppose you were fat?'

'I'll never be fat,' was her answer. I have often wondered if she ever has been.

There was Stella too, a fiery red-head, who lived in one of the keeper's cottages in the park. She could put on a spectacular display of fireworks if teased sufficiently, but I found it distressing.

Christine lived in a house in the grounds of the City of London cemetery. There were beautiful chestnut trees, and Daddy would often take us for a walk there. Death held no fear for him, so I trust that it was the same for Christine. I called at her home on one occasion.

If we walked through the cemetery we came to a brook lined by alder trees. It was from this that our estate, Aldersbrook, got its name.

Then suddenly I lost all my friends for Mr. Lindley, for some reason, decided to remove me from my class and place me in the next one up where he was now teaching. You can imagine that these older children did not welcome me with open arms, and it was an unhappy experience for me, for I had little enough confidence as it was. These juniors had already mastered the mysteries of long multiplication and long division and I had to catch up. Mr. Lindley called me to his desk and went through the intricacies with me, but I was none the wiser. It was my poor mother who was left to teach me. What would I have done without her?

Then one day the door opened and in came Janice. She was the daughter of a bank manager and lived in one of the 'posh' detached houses on the main road. Was it because of the war that she had been taken from the private school she had been attending? She was put to sit beside me. I would not be without a friend now, though I was not always appreciative of it.

My mother received a note from Janice's mother saying how grateful she was that her daughter had such a nice friend and inviting me to tea. From then on there was no escape. Her parents were lovely to me. Cars were rare in those days but they had a little Austin 7. Jezebel, they called her, but she never let us down when I was in her, and I was included in many a family outing, even a holiday in a sailing cruiser on the Norfolk Broads.

They should have been wonderful days for me, but I felt that I was under Janice's domination, and try as I would I could not be myself. We had gone on to High school now and were playing in a copse that was out of bounds. It was not in my nature to break the rules but where she went I had to follow.

'Go on, jump! I promise you that if you do this, I'll never ask you to do anything again.'

It may not have been more than six or seven feet but it seemed more to me. I was terrified, but if this should break her domination of me then I must do it. I jumped, but alas, she did not keep her word.

I am sure that she did not mean to be unkind, and felt that she was doing it all for my good, for I was a timid little thing. I had been put into an 'A' stream class because I was a Thompson and expected to be as bright as my brother and sister, and with only just keeping my head above water in my school work and these other pressures I was ill. I know I had swollen glands among other things and was off school for a few weeks.

My mother must have gone to the school to see Miss Alcock who was head of the girls. I returned to find I had been put in a lower class. I felt loved and accepted there and apart from the trauma of exams, (I was a terrible worrier,) I think I quite enjoyed school. Janice lost interest in me after that.

Of course we had our own friends in the Bible Students. I remember at one time we had Sunday School around our dining room table, with our dear Uncle Ted as our teacher. John had his great friend Derrick whom we adored, then there was Ruth, about my age, and David, who lived in our old house in Woodlands Avenue and the three Evans girls and Rosemary, who had an older sister. Have I forgotten others? It was to Rosemary's house that we were invited to watch the Coronation, my first experience of television. We children grew up together, and sometimes would have a picnic and fun and games in the park. There was a wonderful bond between us. Dad had made sure that we all had a bicycle as soon as war was declared, in case of invasion, though I don't know where we would have fled to if the Germans had landed. You couldn't buy new bicycles by then, but someone put some old ones together. I remember Janice teaching me to ride. No matter how many were my bruises I had to get up and try again. Yet I am grateful to her that I learned, for we youngsters had many an outing up to Buckhurst Hill where Derrick lived, and from there into Epping Forest.

One year we went on holiday with our bicycles. We left early in the morning so that we could take them on the underground across London and then cycled from there out into Wiltshire. We have often laughed about the return journey. John was way ahead of us, but suddenly we saw him cycling toward us, head down, on the other side of the dual carriageway. He had gone right round a roundabout by mistake. You should have seen his face when we shouted to him.

Our group of Bible Students were now meeting in the Labour Hall in Ilford, but the 'Forest Gate' group as we called them were meeting in the Bowling Club at the end of our road. There must have been some differences in doctrine but I don't know if I ever knew what they were. As we got older we had more to do with their young people and had some wonderful times together.

But now I was growing up and these friendships could not stay on the same level. I was fourteen, and had reached the trauma of puberty, when you seem to be a mixture of personalities. John had gone away to university, and probably because he had lost his best friend, Derrick wanted to have a closer relationship with me.

Of course I loved him, and was flattered. I remember when I was at college Ethel teased me that I was so sweet that I would say yes to the first person who asked me. I know I told Derrick that 'I could never say no.'

I was much too immature to cope with such a relationship and my parents were very unhappy about it. It brought a rift in their friendship with his parents for a while, but in the end we all agreed that it was better for us to part. I had a tremendous sense of relief, but I suffered from nervous headaches and my parents bought me a little dog, Laddie, to help me to get over it.

When Derrick found another girl friend, a beautiful blond and far more mature than I, I wept inconsolably, but I think it was more for fear that I might be left on the shelf than because I really loved

him, for I had one ambition, to be married and have six children.

We heard no teaching of salvation but we were taught that we should consecrate our lives to God and be baptised in water. It must have been after John and Derrick were baptised that I felt that I wanted to be the same, but I thought it meant being good. Whatever my resolutions I could never keep it up for long.

I loved devotional poetry, and one Sunday night I had stayed at home; I don't remember why. All I know is that I had felt the pressure of a great love and knew that I must surrender my life to God. When my parents came in I told them that I had consecrated my life to God. Mary had made the same decision just prior to this and we were baptised in water in the large Baptist church just up the road from the Labour Hall.

I loved the Lord as much as I knew him, and certainly we all lived an exemplary devotional life, but it was some years before I knew Jesus as my Saviour. But now I had to think of a career, though I had little idea of how important this was, and how it would lead to this great journey, on the wings of the morning.

CHAPTER SEVEN—COLLEGE DAYS

'Now then, pick up your pencils. That's right. Now, pencils down.' The head mistress was supposed to be giving a model lesson, for I was a prospective teacher. Suddenly she strode across the room and rapped a child on the wrist. 'Laura, I said pencils down.'

'Oh, I'm sorry, Miss Vose.'

We thought the incident was over, but a minute or two later the child came out in floods of tears.

'I'm ever so sorry, Miss Vose.'

'That's all right, dear. I have forgiven you.'

'Yes, but I'm ever so sorry I've wet my knickers. You gave me such a fright that I couldn't help it.' The poor thing was duly sent off to be changed.

That is one of the first amusing incidents that I recall from my teaching days. I had no idea of what I wanted to do with my life, except that it had to be something with children, probably because I felt safe with them.

'Of course you must go into teaching,' our Senior Mistress had said. She arranged for me to go for a month to an Infant school to see how I got on, and this is where I had my experience of delightful, old fashioned teaching. Alas, such methods were soon to be exchanged for organised chaos, where the children were supposed to learn through play. I observed, and taught some lessons as part of my training, but then one of the teachers was away and I was thrown in the deep end. I was not too impressed with my efforts, but the teacher, when she returned, had heard otherwise, and she told me this. 'Never cry stinking fish.' It is something I try to remember.

So now it was confirmed that I was to teach. I did have six weeks at the nursery of the infamous Aldersbrook Homes, my first opportunity to earn some money. Though we were caring for babies under eighteen months the place was run as a hospital. Can you imagine potting twenty babies all at the same time and all screaming their heads off? The whole regime was heart breaking, but I was quite ready to make this work my career. It was my mother who insisted that I go on to college and have some qualification behind me, though she had missed out on this herself.

There had been no talk of me going to university, though John had just got his science degree at Leeds, and we were very proud that Mary had gained a scholarship to Cambridge. I always had to struggle with my school work, though I gained my 'Matric' as we called it with eight or was it nine passes, and several credits.

Miss Alcock had told me that I didn't have a chance of passing at Latin, though she admitted that I worked as hard as anyone, but I set out to disprove her and somehow I did.

To my mother's relief, exams had lost their terror for me when I was in the sixth form for although I was sitting for my 'A' levels, - Higher, I think we called it then, I had already been accepted into teacher training college, whether I passed or not. I asked to give up French after a few months so that I could take up music again.

I didn't have an aptitude for languages, which makes my future efforts all the more wonderful. I learned French for six years and when I met a French boy I didn't understand a word. Mind you, I think he had gabbled on purpose. Then of course there was the embarrassing incident when I had forgotten that 'tiroir' was the word for drawer, so looked it up in the dictionary. Here I found it already in the plural for me. Alas, it was drawers of another kind!!!

We had all had music lessons with our cousin, Marguerite, older than us and now a professional teacher, but I must have been a trial to her. The other three took to the piano like a duck to water but I never could remember in which key I was supposed to be playing. I begged my mother to let me give up and have elocution lessons instead. I so wanted to be an actress. I was allowed to give up music but I never had my elocution lessons. But now I went to a neighbour. I do remember that I had some singing lessons with her at one time. It was after I had mumps, to help me to get my poor mouth open again. She told my mother that I could only improve!! It was Joy who should have had singing lessons. She so loved music. She had our old wind up gramophone working whenever she could and would be singing all day long.

Mrs. Smith's few piano lessons were a great help to me when I began teaching. My voice has never been strong, and it was such a help with the little children to sit at the piano and get them to sing or march. There was a special tune for making them quiet too. Very useful. But now the days were drawing near for me to go to college. It was the first time for me to be away from home on my own and I was scared. It had never entered my head that I might enjoy it, as school had not been a happy experience, though life was good in the sixth form. I was a prefect now. We had some girls come to us from the convent, and they thought that I was a confident person. Imagine! Me! On the whole, I did enjoy college, and of course it was the means of leading me into a new dimension of living, and to setting out on the wings of the morning.

There were books to buy, new clothes to be made, or bought. At last the day came when with trepidation I set out, my family seeing me off from Liverpool Street station. My cabin trunk, and bicycle were stacked into the guard's van and I was on my way. We had to change at Audley End, and take the branch line to the little market town of Saffron Walden and here I found I was not alone, and strangely it was not as terrifying as I had thought. 'I say, have you met Esther? Come on, she lives on North.'

I was rooming in the hostel for the first two terms. It was a draughty old house, and there were four of us in a room. At one time we had an invasion of mice. That caused some excitement, if not hysteria.

The college was interdenominational so most of us were from some sort of Christian background, but the 'real' Christians soon found each other, and there was a Christian Union. CU we called it. I remember telling someone about the doctor who had come to CU. She insisted that no doctor had come to see her. For a long time we were at cross purposes.

Esther's Auntie Lois also came and spoke to us. A wonderful Christian, who had been a missionary in China for many years, I have never forgotten her message.

Rose was a lovely Christian, from a Closed Brethren background, which she later renounced. She was the only one I knew, apart from myself, who did not go to the college dance, though I found others afterwards. She was a comfort to me.

I shared with Eileen and Ethel in my second term, and they have become life long friends, though it is all due to their faithfulness. My experience with Janice as well as my religious persuasion, made me very wary of becoming involved with anyone.

But now Ethel insisted that I must come and meet Esther. She was a load of fun. 'Come in!' I looked to see where the voice had come from and eventually located her, perched on the back of her chair with a book in her hand.

Esther was different. Striking rather than pretty, with her plaited hair crowning her head, she had a quick wit and excelled at whatever she did. She had come to college in order to equip herself for missionary work, though I had no idea of this at the time, and it was only later that I learned of the tragedy of her mother's death through cancer. She was one of the very few who didn't put on weight at college. We were out in the open air so much with our environmental studies and sport activities that we developed huge appetites. There was still rationing, though the war had now been over four years, but the college food was good, and there were always second helpings. Saturday mornings we had to clean our rooms and then we would wander into town and sometimes indulged in coffee and cream doughnuts, though money was tight for those of us who didn't get a grant. I was supported by my parents. Most of us put on weight. They used to tease me that I was a 'dear little round thing,' but Esther was one of Pharoah's lean kine.

I didn't have much to do with her at college. She was Ethel's friend, but I shall never forget the first time I heard her sing. 'Choral' on a Monday evening was something we all enjoyed, whether we were musical or not. If I sat next to Ethel I could hold the alto parts. Miss Rolph was quite ugly in appearance, but she was one of the most beautiful characters I have met. With a child like enthusiasm she taught us to love music and we all loved her. We sang the St. Matthew's Passion and the Christmas Oratorio in the beautiful Anglican church in the town, with students from Cambridge taking the men's parts.

Now, as we met to practice I heard Esther's voice soaring, like a boy soprano, as she took the solo part, 'With verdure clad.'

But I didn't have much to do with her. How little did I know what an important part she would have in the shaping of my life, preparing me to go forth, on the wings of the morning.

'Tell me, what did you enjoy most of all about college?' I was being interviewed now as a prospective teacher. My answer was spontaneous. 'Oh, having a room of my own, and yet plenty of company.'

That was in our second year. Ethel was next door and Esther across the corridor. We had plenty of open air life, and we used to adorn our rooms with flowers we had picked from the hedge rows. They used to go up to Eileen's room for a prayer meeting. I went sometimes but I don't think I kept it up for long. I didn't really belong to them, because of our Bible Student teaching. I wanted to be friendly with the more worldly girls, but I didn't belong to them either.

Ethel used to take me along to the Baptist church where Mr. Blower, the minister, made us college girls very welcome. Esther was preaching one Sunday. I was very impressed at her oratory. But then I went again and it was Trinity Sunday. Oh dear, that didn't suit a Bible Student.

'Oh do come. It's really meant for people like you.' Ethel was very insistent, and against my better judgement I went along to a special communion service. But we Bible Students only took the Communion once a year, at the time of the Passover. The Memorial we called it. I was given permission to go home for this, one year when it didn't coincide with our holidays. It was very special and we would spend the whole day meditating and preparing ourselves. But now here I was, expected to partake in the Baptist church. I didn't have the sense to let the emblems pass me by. I took a piece of bread. It was in my pocket for weeks. I didn't like to throw it away. And the deacons must have wondered why there was still a glass of wine left in the pew.

'I know what you are. You're a Jehovah's Witness.' She was a sweet young Christian that we had met at the church and had invited us back to her home, but she accused me with venom. I insisted that I was not, and dear Ethel stuck up for me, but of course she was right. Though separated from them, much of our doctrine was that still held by the JWs.

I remember at school there were a few evangelical Christians who were heroic in their efforts to witness. I did my best to avoid getting into discussion with them, and was so convinced that they were in error. I remember Pam had read a book about JW doctrine, and told me things that I did not know we believed, but later I found she was right. But I was so deeply embedded in this doctrine. However was it possible that I could be changed?

Before I close this chapter about college I must mention teaching practice.

'Excuse me, how old are you?' The child was very polite and I told him, 'Nineteen.' He proceeded to pass the word around, 'Teacher's ninety.'

The village school could have been taken out of one of the 'Miss Reid' books. I loved it, especially when the class teacher, who was a bit of a dragon and resented the disruption of students, was away for a few days, and my lecturers were pleased. I thought I would have loved to have lived and taught in a village like this, but of course it was impossible because of my fear of spiders and creepy crawlies. It was when I was teaching in a village in New Guinea that I realised that in this too God had given me the desires of my heart.

I did have a bad report on one occasion. I was devastated, and felt that I would never be able to teach again. I had the class working in groups when the art lecturer had descended on me. Three quarters of the class were working industriously, but of course she only noticed the ones who were not. Too late I realised that the activity I had planned for them was not a success, but could not do much about it so let them carry on. Most of our lecturers were helpful and understanding, but not this one. However, my dear friends helped to pick up the pieces and put me together again.

Then we each had a subject in which we specialised. Esther took New Testament Greek. She had special tuition from the Vicar. One sunny day I thought there was a persistent bumble bee outside my window until I went to her room and found her seated on her window sill, reading aloud.

I chose religious knowledge, and did a study of the Apostle Peter. I so loved writing this, and also the environmental study that I did of Epping Forest. I suppose this was a beginning of my writing.

Esther

CHAPTER EIGHT—HOXTON

'I was a student at your college many years ago, and wondered whether any of your students would like to come to my school.'

The letter, addressed to our principal, had been placed on the college noticeboard. I had already applied to teach in Suffolk, but the weekend I had to make the decision my father had been very ill and I felt that I should not leave home. Miss Schroder, the writer of this letter, mentioned that her children were in a needy area, and she was looking for dedicated teachers. I decided to apply. Some time after,I heard that Esther too had been accepted to go to the same school. She lived in Surrey and I in Essex, but between us lay Hoxton. Only God could have planned this.

'Excuse me, but are you a lady or a girl?' It was my first day, and I was shepherding my children into the classroom.

The junior boy standing there was genuinely puzzled. I was always taken to be much younger than I was, probably because of my lack of confidence. 'I hope I am a lady,' I tried to reply with dignity. Of course, later on I learned otherwise.

'Lady! lady!' Leslie's small cousin had come to meet him and was calling to me from the door.

'Be quiet!' commanded Leslie, 'She ain't a lady, she's a teacher. Calling you a lady,' he smiled apologetically.

Hoxton used to have a very bad reputation. There was a time when policemen would never go there unaccompanied. If he was unwanted a manhole might be removed and he dumped into it. That was years ago, but even so, we never liked to go to the other end of the market when we had our lunch time walk, and when our school was removed to that end of the street there was often a sinister atmosphere. There was the case of the foreman who was supervising some building who had his life threatened by the local workmen, and one day I had to go to fetch a child's mother and found no one on the usually busy street except one man who was threatening another with a butcher's cleaver.

It was an experience teaching these needy children. I began with forty five under fives, and felt that nothing I had been taught at college had prepared me for this.

Hoxton

'What is your name?' I asked one boy, trying to match up the list in the register. 'Ballyclillyardenouse,' was his reply. I later translated this into, 'Barry Crilley,' and his address, 'Arden House.' But then a good angel came to my rescue. Mrs. Harris, our 'helper' arrived and we pinned names to the children. Knowing who they were made all the difference, and I gradually came to understand their cockney too. We had the Station (salvation) Army and station (alsatian) dogs in Hoxton, and 'my dad says if he 'its me I've got'a 'it 'im raand the ear 'ole.'

I was non plussed when the head mistress, checking through the absentees with me declared that they were hopping. Was that another expression for playing truant? Then one rainy playtime I had left the class for a few minutes and returned to find they had piled as much furniture as they could onto the sand trolley and were pushing it happily round the room.

When I asked what they thought they were doing they told me, 'We're going 'opping.' I learned that many of the East Enders loaded as much of their possessions as they could onto lorries or carts and went to Kent for the summer to work in the hop fields.

The Cockneys had a ripe vocabulary, but fortunately perhaps, many of their swear words failed to shock me. I had no idea of what they were saying. But for John, everything was 'bloody' and I did object to that. I waited until I had him alone. 'Teacher, they're painting the bloody fence,' he told me. 'Are they painting it red?' I asked. 'Then is there blood on it?' Again he shook his head. 'Well, aren't you silly saying it is bloody when it isn't.' He never used the word again, in my hearing, anyway.

They had a wonderful cockney humour. Once I found they had been throwing sand. They were sat in disgrace while I tried to clear up the mess. 'Look, sand in this - and sand in that.' I took off my sandal to shake sand out of that when Jimmy said, 'And the sand has made a hole in teacher's stocking.' That put an end to my tirade.

I was determined that my children would want to come to school, and it was wonderful how within a month a mob had become a manageable class.

Like me, Miss Schroder was not the greatest of disciplinarians, but she loved the children. She and Miss Turner, her deputy, had been teaching for forty years in the same area and parents brought their children from far a field to come to her school.

Wings of the Morning

We learned so much from these wise women as they shared their stories in the staff room.

'If the children need a smack you give it to them,' Miss Schroder told us, 'and I'll stick up for you if there's trouble.' Even in those days you might be taken to court for smacking, and every caning had to be recorded in a black book. Usually it only needed one smack, so that they learned that you meant what you said, and Miss Turner had told us what to say to children who threatened to tell their Dad. 'You tell him. I would like to see your Dad to tell him what a naughty boy (or girl) you are.' You could be sure that they wouldn't after that.

There was an occasion when Jimmy 'Doodle' did tell his Mum, and she sailed into school 'ready to have my liver and lights,' but fortunately for me she accused the wrong teacher.

The children were very needy. It wasn't so long since they had had boot clubs, and they still had flower competitions, when they were given bulbs to grow at home, to brighten up their lives. They brought them back to be judged.

'Mine's the best, 'cos my Dad gave it the dregs of 'is beer,' one child told us.

Many had free dinners, though some of those who had to pay a shilling preferred to keep the money and go to the pie shop for eel pie and liquor.

There were so many extra duties beside teaching. Counting up the dinner money was a nightmare as the children paid according to their number in their family. I would just learn to add up in sevenpence halfpennies when they would change the price.

One day I called out the children who had to pay for their cod liver oil and malt. Tina, who was well named, wept bitterly because I told her she was free. 'I'm not free, I'm five.'

It was a great day when instead of the awful spoonfuls of the gooey stuff we gave out capsules. There was milk too. It was some years later when, instead of bottles they had three cornered cartons. One elderly supply teacher told us her classroom was like Canaan's land, flowing with milk and honey.

One morning I was trying to bundle up the laundry besides all my other duties. Some children were waiting to carry the sack across to the caretaker and were chatting among themselves. Suddenly they asked me, 'Teacher, why don't you go out to work? Our Mums do.'

When I spoke of my own mother, they laughed. 'You haven't got a mummy,' they told me. 'You are a mummy,' and wanted to know about my 'daddy', my husband.

They were convinced that I lived in the school and to many I was giving the security they lacked in their home life.

'Miss Thompson, will you marry me when I'm grown up?' I had many a proposal, and felt quite safe in promising that if they still wanted to when they were grown up, then I would.

My mother loved the story about Arthur. It was 'speech training.' 'I think I can, I think I can,' chugged the engine going up the hill. Over my shoulder I heard Arthur, 'I fink I can, I fink I can.'

I turned to him. 'Arthur, think!'

'All right, don't spit.'

All of the older teachers were old maids, for it was only as a result of the war that teachers were allowed to continue after they were married. There was some jealousy and backbiting, but Miss Dengate never joined in. She had a club foot, an invalid sister, and did a long train and bus journey each day, and then coped with these lively East Enders. Usually placid, you knew she was near the end of her tether if you heard her call her children 'sausages.' I was shocked when by mistake I opened her pay slip. I was then receiving twenty seven pounds a month, and though nearing retirement, her pay was only thirty five.

But Miss Dengate had a secret joy, her cats. She used to walk home across one of the derelict bomb sights that still remained after the war though the scars were now softened by the blush of rose bay willow herb that had sprung up. Having collected all the scraps from our school dinners, she would feed the stray cats that had set up home there. They lived wild and no one else could get near them, but they would come to her. It was a sad day for her when the van had been round to get rid of the cats, but she always found that one or two survived and soon had a family again.

Esther never had any problems with discipline, but though I loved it, I never found teaching easy. Maybe I have a special ministry to encourage others who also find it hard.

Because of my own unhappy experience at school I was determined that if I did nothing else that I would see that my children wanted to come to school. But one day I was in despair.

'Lord,' I prayed, 'I can't teach these children.'

'But will you love them for me?'

'Yes, Lord, if you will help me, I will love them for you.'

What had happened? I had prayed, and God had answered me. He did help me to love them and the children responded. There was poor little John who could not say a word. The day came when he stood, tugging my sleeve and saying 'pa-per.' He wanted to paint. It was a break through, and he eventually began to read. He would even choose a song. 'Hum dum,' was his favourite, (Humpty Dumpty.)

'Do you know why we all got gold stars?' Gary asked. Gary suffered from asthma, and was so anxious to please that he usually got things wrong.

'No. Why?'

"cos we asked Jesus to help us.' Bless him, I found they were having a little prayer meeting before they started their work. I hadn't preached, just told them the Bible stories, and he had known that this Jesus was for him too.

Then there was Sotty Raggy. His real name was Sotirios, but if I called him that then he knew he was in trouble. We did not have a good impression of his father but Sotty had found someone else to befriend him.

We had been talking about the policeman, the nurse, - friends in the community. Now they had to draw a picture.

'Who is that, Sotty?' It was a man in a top hat.

'That's God, 'cause he's my friend.' I found that the other children were almost jealous of his relationship.

'Isn't God our father too? Well Sotty says he is his father.'

It wasn't all success. Far from it. There was a verse in the Psalms that I felt was especially for me, 'Who subdues the people under me.' I often had to claim it, but though I would be like a cloth that has been wrung out at the end of term I loved working with these needy children and felt it was so worth while, and it was in those early years of teaching that there had been a wonderful change in my life. I had found a relationship with God that for all my religious experience I had never known before.

Hoxton

CHAPTER NINE—NEW LIFE

Esther didn't stay at Hoxton House, as our school was called, for with the long journey and pressures in her personal life, after four years she had a break down and got a job nearer home. I suppose she was there as long as God had needed her to be used to bring about this wonderful change in my life.

Not that she preached at me. She didn't. Nor did I ever feel that she was pressurising me, though she was, is, a very strong character. In many ways she reminded me of Janice, yet never did I feel that she was dominating me, and gradually my defences were down and we became close friends.

The first occasion I went to her home was for her and Sheila's twenty first birthday party, when I met her father, dignified and gracious, with a quick wit and a loving heart, and dear little Rose, Rowie we called her, Esther's step mother. I was soon to become one of the family. Her 'adopteds' Rowie came to call Mary and me, and we couldn't have been loved more.

John was now working in Leeds as a pest control officer, and Joy was farming. She wanted to get as far away from the family as she could. It must have been difficult to be the last of the little Thompsons. We still laugh at the time she came home crying because Mr. Lindley had told her she was the 'little black pig' of the family, but it must have been very hard for her to be constantly compared with her brother and sisters, even if he had said black sheep.

Soon after Mary finished at college she was courting, and I began to join the Knights for holidays.

To me holidays meant being by the sea, but they loved walking in the countryside, and it always seemed to rain. Was it our first holiday when we went to Lynton? It certainly rained then. It was the year of the terrible floods when the river burst its banks and lives were lost. As we stood beside the concrete foundations that were all that were left of peoples homes, I noticed a child's toy, somehow left behind as the torrent swept onward, a lonely symbol of a life that was no more.

'If I love the Lord, and you love him, then surely God will lead us in the same way?' I had been reading 'The Christian's Secret of a

Happy Life,' and the author had said that we should ask God, that if there was something wrong in our lives, he would put it right. I had done this, so was disappointed when Esther didn't think it possible. Of course she was well aware of the great differences in our beliefs. But God did it all the same.

The guest house where we had stayed in Lynton was Pentecostal. The Knights weren't Pentecostal either, being staunch members of an evangelical church. I thought that these different ways of worshipping were according to our different natures, and that the exuberance of Pentecostals certainly wasn't for me.

After all these years it is hard to remember how the change in me took place, but I know that it did, and that is what matters.

Billy Graham came to London. It was 1952, and the first Harringay Crusade. All of London was agog. Esther and her family were involved in counselling and many of us Bible Students went out of curiosity. Of course Billy Graham, like the rest of the denominations, was in error, so we believed, and yet we found God in those great meetings. This was not something that we could sweep aside. I believe that some of the young people of the more open Bible Students went forward for salvation. We didn't go that far. I was convinced that I was right with God, but we did start a prayer meeting in 'Uncle' Ted's home and it was there that I began to find the power there was in prayer.

It must have been around this time that John encouraged me to become more involved with the 'Forest Gate' young people and now we were all going on with God.

In 1953 they were preparing for another Billy Graham crusade, and I received a letter inviting me to the training sessions for counsellors.

How had this miracle happened, that I, a Bible Student, should be welcomed? There was a simple explanation. The previous counsellors had all been enrolled in a course where they undertook to commit to memory so many verses from the Bible. I used to see Esther learning her texts each day, and thought that I would like to do the same. Hence my name had got onto their mailing list. Learning the Bible verses too must have been changing me.

Now as I went to these training classes I sat under the ministry of Lorne Sanny. He spoke of being born again, and how we must know that we have had this experience. I had no doubt that I was a

Christian, that the Lord Jesus Christ was my Saviour, and that he had died for me. When had it happened?

Then I recalled how I had been in bed, reading Roy Hession's book, 'The Calvary Road.' I had known that I did things that were wrong and would ask for forgiveness, but I had been taught that it was Adam who was to blame. Now as I read I realised for the first time that if no one else had sinned, that Jesus would have needed to have gone to the cross to bring me to God. My sin was that of the lost sheep. I had been going my own way, but now I wanted to go his. I knelt by my bed and prayed the prayer that was written there,

'Lord, bend this proud, stiff neck-ed I,
Help me to bow the head and die,
Beholding him on Calvary
Who bowed his head for me.'

I didn't know that this was getting saved, and that anything special had happened in my life, but looking back I realised that it was from then on that I had a peace and joy that I had never known before.

I had often prayed that God would take me to heaven, because I had thought that I would be happy there, for I had weak nerves like my father and often suffered from depression. I didn't get an instant cure, but I was happy now in a way I had never been before.

Our only outreach in the Bible Students had been giving out tracts. 'Tracking' they used to call it, to our amusement. We didn't do any of the aggressive door knocking, but even so, I was terrified lest someone would come to the door when I put something through their letter box.

I still don't have courage to go and accost someone, but I knew now that I had a message that they needed, and I wanted them to know this wonderful Saviour who had become the centre of my life.

I think that was the difference. God had been somewhere on the outside before, but now he was in the centre. When my thoughts came to rest, they rested on him.

The Bible came alive to me. Mind you, it was no wonder I hadn't read it much before. I still had the little pocket Bible that 'Auntie Warnes' had given me when I was seven. Now John gave me a lovely large study Bible and I found it was a living word.

One day I came home having visited 'Auntie Em.' Recently bereaved of both her husband and father, she was in deep distress and had come out in terrible sores all over her legs. I opened my Bible to read the words, 'I will bind up the broken in heart and heal their wounds.' I knew this was a promise I could claim. Many times it seemed the Bible had been written just for me.

But I think it was the children who taught me that you don't have to be miserable, even if you have sinned. When I had to punish them they knew I was still their friend, and I realised I had to have the same confidence in God.

I went to Lowestoft for a holiday with Auntie Joan and my younger cousins. I had been so involved I had forgotten to read my Bible or pray. How could I now come to God? Suddenly I realised, that was just the reason I needed to come.

'O Saviour, I have naught to plead,
On earth below or heaven above
Except my own exceeding need
And thy exceeding love.'

We young people had started to go into the park for an open air service on a Sunday afternoon. Oh yes, Lord, I would speak, but I must be sure that you want me to. Let someone ask me, so that I may be sure.

'Pauline, why don't you speak. Go on!' It was old brother Stokes. How could he know the Lord's will? I didn't obey.

I was wretched for a day or two, then I told the Lord. 'All right, now you know what a failure I am. I can't do it, but you can.'

I knew that God was answering my prayer when, the following week, in the prayer meeting prior to our going our they asked for those who were prepared to speak. There was no getting out of it now. I had great joy in giving his word, and did on many other occasions.

Meanwhile there were great changes going on in Esther's life. Her family had been brought in contact with some members of the Apostolic Church and felt such conviction that the revelation they brought them was of God that they left their local fellowship and began to hold house meetings. Esther had been through her own battles to come to this step of faith, but I knew little of this at the time. I was going through deep waters myself, for it is very hard to break away from teaching in which you have been brought up. I felt as if I were struggling through thick cloud, and depression.

We were on holiday at Heathfield when some words came to my mind, something about 'blue skies will soon be o'er you, where the dark clouds have been.' I didn't even know if it was a hymn, or if it could be true, but I held on to it.

Another time I was seated in a bus when the verse came clearly to me, 'The blessing of the Lord it maketh rich, and addeth no sorrow.' Somehow I knew that eventually the struggle would be over, and that God would not lead me astray.

Wonderful things began to happen. I went with Esther to the Apostolic church in Kennington on a Thursday evening. They were singing a hymn I had never heard before, 'A wonderful Saviour is Jesus my Lord,' and I felt I had come home.

I was scared of these spiritual gifts Esther talked about, but there was nothing at first, only when Miss Morgan prayed I thought the roof of the building had come off and the heaven was open.

I would go home with Esther sometimes for their Wednesday meeting, which was now in Ethel White's home. One night Pastor W.H.Lewis, one of the early pioneers in our fellowship, was the minister.

'I don't know why, but I feel I must leave my notes and speak on the Divinity of Christ.' On another occasion the same thing happened, and he spoke of the Personality of the Holy Spirit. He didn't know of my background, but God did, and was teaching me more of himself.

Then there was the time when I did hear spiritual gifts; men speaking words that came from the heart of God, and they dared to say, 'Thus saith the Lord.'

I remember the word, 'There are some among you that are not as you think.' It was true. I had always come with Esther, and they thought I was a good little evangelical as she was, but God knew all about me.

I was given a precious word, that the Lord would lay his hand on me, that at times I would feel that it was too heavy for me to bear, but that through the pressure there would be release of life to those who were bound. I still claim that word, but at that time I was beginning to feel the pressure.

I was going to these meetings and knew that God was there, and I was still going to the Bible Student meetings, and hearing the teaching which I had always been told was 'the Truth.'

It had been so easy to believe as they did. Everyone would be resurrected in the Millennium and then they would come to believe in Jesus. But was this in the Bible?

While working with the young people I had prepared a Bible study, in which we had sought to come afresh and see what the Bible really did say. I found that it said that now is the day of salvation, that it is appointed to men, once to die and after that the judgment.

What was I to believe?

One night, in desperation, I cried out, 'Lord, it was so easy for your disciples. They just had to follow Jesus, but I am having to find out what is right and what is wrong.'

Deep in my spirit God answered me. 'No, it is just the same for you. It is just for you to follow Jesus.'

'Lord, if that is really true, then make it so plain for me that it is either to follow you or to deny you.' Could he answer my prayer?

A Portrait. I am twenty-one.

CHAPTER TEN—SEPARATION

'For me, to go to meetings where they deny that Jesus is God, would be to deny my Lord.' It was a direct answer to my prayer.

Though Esther was away that weekend, I had come to Carshalton as I so often did and now I was sitting in the front room with her parents.

There had been no pastor in the little cottage meeting that morning, no one with spiritual gifts, but the Lord had been so near, and there had been one theme, that of separation.

'I know God was speaking to me,' I confided, 'but I don't know what he wants me to do.' It was then that dear 'Uncle Harry' made the issue plain for me and I knew now that I would never go back.

It was the hardest decision I have ever made in my life, for I knew that it would bring pain to so many who were dear to me.

I went on from Carshalton to spend a few days holiday with my aunt, Nesta. She couldn't understand why I had to leave the Bible Students to join a little known Pentecostal church, but there was no other choice. God had not only led me out, but led me in.

We had been the ideal Bible Student family, and now they thought that I had 'gone to the devil' in joining a Pentecostal church.

It was a hard time. I used to be fearful of meeting any of the Bible Students, and now I began to attend the little Apostolic Church in Barking, for I couldn't cross London every Sunday to go to Carshalton, but I was just as scared to go there.

Some of the Bible Students tried to excuse me by suggesting that I had joined this church because there were more young people there, but this was far from the case. There had never been any shortage of young men in the Bible Students and I don't know of any of the girls who failed to get a husband. Now, at twenty four, most of the eligible Apostolics had already been snapped up.

The smallest church building in Barking, they were mostly elderly folk who attended there, and some of them were what we used to call Pentecostal with a capital P. Saved under the ministry of Stephen Jeffreys, they would not only speak in tongues, but shiver and shake and I wondered what I had come into.

One day dear Pastor W.H. Lewis and his wife were there and he said, 'I'm sure that you will find this your spiritual home.' I didn't think it possible but it happened.

One evening we sang the hymn, 'I am thine, Lord Jesus, Ever thine. thine I am, And my heart is singing, glory to the Lamb.' As we sang my heart was warmed and I was filled with a joy that overcame the fear.

But something else wonderful had happened. The Lord had been dealing with my problem of jealousy.

My parents had believed it was wrong to praise children. If someone spoke well of me my Mother would compare me unfavourably with Mary, in her absence of course. It was no wonder I was jealous.

I was sorry for myself that I had this problem of jealousy and inferiority, until the Lord showed me that I must acknowledge that these things were sin; that it was because self was on the throne instead of Christ. I learned that when these feelings attacked me I could claim his saving power. I would sing the hymn, 'Jesus saves me now.' I still have to sing it.

Once I had confessed my need, it was wonderful how the situation changed; as if the Lord was saying that since I had committed it to him, he would see that I had no more excuse to be jealous.

I had dreaded that I might be jealous of Mary in her marriage. I was so relieved that she had married an older man who had no attraction for me. Now, whereas before she had always taken the lead, it was I who had been first to come out of the Bible Students and into the Apostolic church.

I had always had great difficulty in expressing myself. Many of our meetings were open Bible studies, but if I ever took part, no one seemed to understand what I was trying to say. I had felt such a coward that so much was being said that I did not now agree with and yet I was silent. I dreaded arguments, and so now God had given me this opportunity to speak by my actions. By coming out from them, every one now knew what I believed.

For a few weeks Mary continued to meet with the Bible Students. She had wonderful opportunities to speak her faith. Then she was away with her husband on holiday.

Separation

One Thursday night I returned home from Barking feeling burdened with the pressure of rejection and misunderstanding. I arrived home to find Mary would be with us for a few days.

She had been going through rough waters in her marriage. Her husband had had a break down, and had wanted to be left alone for a while. Though the circumstances were so sad it was wonderful for me. Having learned to stand on my own, the Lord was now giving me someone to stand with me and it made all the difference.

On the Saturday evening we went to Kennington for a young peoples' rally. I gave my testimony that night, sharing how I had found Jesus himself to be the way, the truth and the life, and Pastor Tom Saunders took it up as he preached on the divinity of Christ.

'Where will you be going tomorrow?' Esther asked Mary. 'Barking,' was her reply. She too had come out.

It was a hard way for her, for now her husband had an excuse, and blamed all their marital troubles onto 'Pentecost' and the Apostolic church, but she had wonderful faith that it would be best for him too in the end.

It was the 19th of January, 1956 that dear Pastor Hadcocks, together with Pastor Angell, received us into fellowship in the little Barking church. It was an assurance to me that it happened on my birthday, and I was so happy that my father had not objected. 'God bless you, my dear,' he said.

My mother too had written to a friend and told her that spiritually I was prospering. She wouldn't have said it to my face.

We learned to love these deeply spiritual women in the church who became mothers in Israel to us and who longed for us to enter into that deeper experience that they had. Esther had already had a mighty experience of the Holy Spirit and talked to me about this, trying to prepare me that sometimes God has to deal with people's reserves so that they might appear to make fools of themselves. But it was Pastor McGill who had made me long for this experience. He told us, 'The Holy Spirit makes Jesus more precious to you.' I wanted this. He had also said, 'It is wonderful to be able to say Hallelujah.' I certainly couldn't. I was so reserved.

Now I began to pray that God would baptise me in his Holy Spirit. I went to a prayer meeting at the Edgware convention specifically to pray for this, but I was scared. What was I expecting? I didn't know. Then Esther put her hand on my shoulder and quietly quoted the verse,

'And His that still small voice we hear, That checks each fault and calms each fear..' I realised then I was not seeking a Stranger, but one who had been abiding in me. I was asking for more of him. The Lord showed me that I had been like a child playing on the shore, happy that I had some of the sea in my bucket, whereas God wanted me to bathe in his fulness. It would not be how much I had of him but that he might have all of me.

We were preparing to go to the Mount, as the little mining village of Penygroes was known to Apostolics, for it was there that they held our annual international convention. Surely God would do something wonderful for me. I was full of expectation.

But it happened before then. I was on my way to the prayer meeting in Barking. It was a beautiful Summer evening and as I walked up the road a great stillness came over my heart. I don't remember one word being spoken in the service, though I suppose it must have been. I was aware only of an overwhelming sense of the presence of God.

For two or three days I had such a sense of awe, an awareness of God's holiness, of a great desire to be clean, and an awareness too of his love for those around me.

I lost this sense of stillness in all the hustle of the train and bus journey to Penygroes but I thought I was in heavenly places as we gathered in the old Temple. We heard a great hallelujah chorus of people praising in the Spirit and listened to Christ exalted through the ministry of the word, and met so many that have become life long friends.

I went along to the tarry meetings, as they were called, expecting some miraculous manifestation but it didn't come there. It was on the golden sands of Rhossilly Bay, in the warm glow of the evening sun that I first spoke one or two syllables of an unknown tongue.

'Will you make a pact with me to read I Corinthians chapter 13 every day for a month?' This had been some time before, and it had been a young man in the Bible Students who had asked me. Had he some ulterior motive?

After catching the train to Liverpool Street on my way to school I would go into St. Botolph's church to pray. As I read this chapter I had gone on to the next verse, 'And covet earnestly the best gifts, and especially that you may prophesy.'

I had no idea at that time what prophecy was, but in simple faith I had prayed that the Lord would give me gifts, and especially prophecy.

Now as I was seeking the fulness of the Spirit I felt again a pressure that I should pray for the gift of prophecy. How dare I ask for it? What a burden I would have to carry, but there was no getting away from it.

I had expected 'tongues' to come in a miraculous way, for them just to bubble out, but it seemed in this initial experience that I had to have them in my mind and then speak them out. It took tremendous faith, but as I obeyed, little by little I received a gift that did bubble up, and is still flowing.

Looking back I realised that I could have had this experience long before.

I was going through a very difficult time at school. I've always been happiest with the reception class, but now with workmen wreaking havoc around us and a difficult class of seven year olds and a new head mistress who was not very understanding, I felt I was at the end of my tether.

I was walking across the playground when this utterance in tongues came out. I laughed. 'You are copying Mrs.Bush.' But it was such a joyous laugh and lifting of my spirit. I Realise now that I hadn't been copying anyone.

It was in a watch night service in our Barking church that I had a beautiful picture come into my mind and I knew that the Lord wanted me to put it into words and speak it out. Afterwards I realised that the Lord had expressed to me a verse of Scripture in this picture.

'You will find that this gift is the most precious thing in your life,' Esther told me, and it was true. How wonderful to be able to speak forth a word from God's heart.

'Every word of God is pure, and he is a shield to those who put their trust in him.' I had gone into the Angells' house to forward their mail for them while they were away, and had taken this verse out of their promise box. I had been so concerned that I might speak a word as from the Lord, but instead that it might be my own imagining. As I read this verse, I knew I could trust God to shield me from all of self.

But I was twenty five. What had happened to the husband and children that I had longed for? And now something else was happening in my life. I was becoming more and more convinced that God was calling me to be a missionary and to work for him abroad.

Pen-y-Groes Convention

CHAPTER ELEVEN—
MISSIONARY CALL

I was still in the Bible Students when God first called me to be a missionary.

It was a beautiful Summer's Sunday evening, and someone was reading the scriptures. 'And Jesus told his disciples, Go out into the villages...'

I don't know how it had happened, but I knew in my heart that God had spoken to me. Having no concept of missionary work abroad, I presumed that God meant the villages of our own land.

The Bowman's were a couple who had a caravan, lived by faith, and preached the Gospel as they understood it in the villages. This was surely what I was to do. My brother John and I were very close at this time and thought we might do this together.

I heard of the Caravan Mission to Village Children. Mary and I went to one of their meetings. Understandably, they welcomed two Bible Students with some suspicion.

Then I was visiting John in Liverpool and his landlady invited us to meet a couple of WEC missionaries who were coming to visit her. It was they who challenged me to consider that God might want me to work for him abroad.

I began to attend the Apostolic church. The first Monday of every month was Missionary Prayer meeting when a letter was read telling of what God was doing through their missionaries all over the world.

In embracing their teaching I didn't have the answer to all my questions, but at least now I didn't have to explain away scriptures. It was God who had led me to take this step of faith and I knew that I could trust him. One day I would understand.

I knew that the great commission was to us, to 'go into all the world and preach the gospel to every creature.' Yes, there was a need in England, but there were the villages in other lands too.

We had 'real live' missionaries come to speak in our churches, Joel with his wife Betty among them. Every time I heard missionaries speak of the need of their field I felt that God was asking me, 'Are you willing to go there?' I would wrestle, thinking of the hardness of the circumstances, but I had to say yes.

Maybe I have to be willing to go there before I can really pray for them, I told myself. God could not be calling me to every land.

'Lord, I'll go anywhere for you, but don't ask me to go on my own.' Yes, I was still hoping for a husband, and in any case, our church did not send single women. But then, in a unique way, Esther went to Nigeria as a missionary.

But how was it that I was still single? Looking back, I blame it onto my great uncle Harry, though a more lovable person you couldn't find.

It was at my grandmother's home. We were out in the yard and I was hiding behind my mother's skirts. Every time I peeped out Uncle Harry would pretend that he was a growly bear. I would scream with excitement. It was a great game, but suddenly my excitement exploded into terror. From then on I had a fear of men, especially those with deep growly voices.

When I reached my teens I was attracted to men of course and I'm sure did my share of running after them, but once they were pursuing me fear would take over and I would flee for my life. I turned away many a prospect of a good marriage but the time of my deliverance was not yet. God doubtless had allowed this, for it was his purpose that I should go out as a single missionary. I was to be 'the little children's mother,' as they called me in New Guinea, the 'Sunday School Mammy' in Ghana, and I could never have fulfilled this calling if I had had a husband and children of my own, but of course I didn't know this at the time.

I was experiencing now God's power to save from sin and fear, but his deliverances did not all come straight away. I had had a terrible fear of spiders and creepy crawlies.

'If you wish to live and thrive,   let a spider run alive,' Dad would tell us, and taking it in his hand would throw it into the garden. If I could only do this they would have no power to frighten me. I had crept up to this tiny creature that was intimidating me, nearer, nearer, to catch hold of it, but terror took over. I was sick and ill in bed.That was years ago. Now surely, as a Christian, I could claim the Lord's victory, but no, I was as bad as ever. In the end I told the Lord, Well, if you want a coward in your service, it's up to you, for I can't do anything about it. It wasn't until I was actually out on the mission field that little by little, the fear went.

But back to my problem with men. A certain gentleman, happily married, probably thought that he would boost my ego by showing that he thought me attractive. Instead I was terrified by his advances. I knew well that it wouldn't be to my advantage, but I insisted that he tell his wife, knowing that if he did he would not dare pester me again. There was forgiveness and reconciliation all round. The matter was over. But no, it wasn't. I had lost my peace. I couldn't eat. I couldn't pray.

'Lord,' I cried, 'Show me what is wrong.' Then the Lord showed me, yes, I had forgiven him, but what about the sin in my life, in thinking such evil thoughts of others?

When I had first known that Christ was my personal Saviour I didn't have any great conviction of sin. I accepted God's word that I had been as a lost sheep, going my own way, and that Jesus had died for me. Now it was as if the Lord gave me a glimpse of the depth of depravity that was in my own heart. I believe that through this experience, trivial and laughable as it may seem to others, the Lord gave me the gift of repentance.

It was after this the Lord began to show me what a beautiful thing is Christian marriage and gave me faith to believe that he had someone for me. I received a prophetic picture of one coming and walking with me into the glory, and then it was confirmed through a word of prophecy in the Penygroes convention, that he wanted us to commit our ways to him and trust him with regard to relationships, that he would bring the right one into our lives.

I believed. Of course he would give me a partner to go as a missionary. But although I longed for marriage I knew that my missionary call must come first.

But how could I go? I wasn't a soul winner even. We were in a youth convention in Barking when I felt the call strongly, but I told the Lord I could not go unless I had led one soul to the Lord.

It was in that same meeting Mary gave her testimony and said that it was through me that she had come to know Christ as Saviour. I had been unaware of this but now God had taken away any excuse.

Pastor Percy John, our missionary secretary, came to Ilford. I had not spoken to anyone of my call but he must have sensed it, for he told me to wait on God and that he would work it out. He would write from time to time to encourage me.

The years were passing. We moved from our five bedroom house at Dover Road to a bungalow in South Woodford, for I was now the only one at home with my parents. I went to teach in Manor Park, still in the East End but nearer home.

But something wonderful had happened before I left Hoxton. I had prayed so much for another Christian teacher to come after Esther left but it seemed the Lord had not answered. We were expecting a new teacher. I was so sure that she would be a Christian, but when she came it was someone I already knew, a lovable girl, but one I would have described as heathen. Then our 'helper' was off for some weeks and of all the mothers she could have chosen, our head asked one I had seen wearing a Scripture Union badge. Saved in a Billy Graham crusade, it was such a joy to get to know her and her family, to hear of the wonderful change in their lives, and to be introduced to the work of the Hoxton Market Mission. God was letting me know that I had not been standing alone but that he had his '7,000' as in Elijah's day.

Esther, home on furlough from Nigeria, tried to encourage me to rest in the Lord concerning my missionary call. The door God had opened for her, in sending her to lecture in the teacher training college in Ilesha, had closed behind her, but he was well able to open another door for me. Part of me was terrified at the thought of going to an unknown situation. I was sure God wouldn't send me where there were mountains and log bridges because I thought he knew I could not cope with that, but still the call was there, pressing upon me. Jesus said, Go ye into all the world and preach the Gospel. Of course, until he sent me forth there was plenty of need and opportunity at home, and I felt fulfilled in teaching, yet God was telling me that I would go forth.

Mark and Lois were a young couple in our church and when Mark's younger sister came to London to teach it was natural that we became friends. We went together to visit her older sister May and her husband, Pastor John Evans, in Dublin. The work was hard there, the atmosphere oppressive, though God was moving, but they took us to Greystones where was a wonderful Protestant lady who ran an orphanage. This was surely a place where I could answer God's call.

I came home and shared my hopes with our pastor James Macey, who had come to Ilford to face a hard situation. 'You are not strong enough to be a missionary,' he told me, but he later admitted to me that at that time the thought of losing one of his most faithful workers had been more than he could bear.

Not strong enough? I would show him. Though I loved teaching I found it drained me. We had the children's work, Sunday School and Hephzibah, a weeknight meeting, as well as other responsibilities in church and when I was at home I could not relax, for Mary's marriage at that time was on the rocks. Her husband was in Ilford, and I lived under the dread of him turning up at home to try to convince our parents that we had 'gone to the devil.'

Not strong enough? I proved the pastor's point, not mine, by having a breakdown.

'I'm very sorry. The injection must have gone to your heart,' the dentist told me. 'It only happens to one in a million.'

How much fear took over, I don't know, but a few weeks later I had another heart attack, and in church, the very place where I trusted for healing.

'You must give up all thought of being a missionary,' the pastor had told me. As I lay, ill in bed, I felt that I must obey. I was biased, after all. Probably he knew best what was God's will for my life. Yet even there I had a ray of hope. I was reading in Hosea 6, and these verses came to me

'On the third day,' day of gladness,
'On the third day,' day of light.
What the day's despair and sighing?
What the darkness of the night?

Third day - day of resurrection,
Day of singing, day of joy.
Jesus Lord, in suffering, dying,
Given to death, to death destroy.

Third day - day of vindication.
All the might and power of God
Brought him to us, Mighty Conqueror,
King of kings and glorious Lord.

Wings of the Morning

On the third day he will raise us,
Though his hand did smite us sore.
Bruised and torn, yet he will heal us,
His life for us evermore.

In his resurrection triumph,
From our loss he'll life bestow.
Divine strength and peace so precious.
All is gain, the Christ to know.

In the power of the third day,
I'll go forth at thy command,
Know, prepared as the morning,
Showers of blessing on the land.
July 1963

For a year I was struggling in health, though I managed to go
back to school after six weeks. Oh yes, and in those six weeks
something wonderful happened. I was sitting in the sunshine, sewing
garments for the orphanage when Pastor Macey came to visit me.

'You should be writing poetry or something.' It was God's
word to me. I began with the 'something,' and wrote some children's
Bible stories. I am sure it helped me to recover, and of course, since
my marriage writing has become a calling too.

But back to this call. It was missionary prayer meeting. We
did not expect spiritual gifts, but the Lord spoke through Jim
McKinley that though I had put away my call, he had not put it away;
that I would go forth, and he promised me joy and peace.

I realised then, that if I had joy and peace I had everything.
But still there was the question, where and how was I to go?

CHAPTER TWELVE—JOYFUL ABANDONMENT

'Are there any young people here with a missionary calling, with either nurses or teaching training, who would offer themselves for the Australian mission fields?'

Pastor Hawkins was a guest speaker at the Penygroes convention. In the missionary meeting I had felt that I had waited long enough and had such a burden that God would open a way for me. There had been a prophetic word, to the effect that through devious paths God would bring us to the place of his will. Then this request came.

I didn't have a specific call for 'down under' but God had asked me to be willing to go anywhere for him. Maybe this would be a step to where God wanted me.

Mary at this time was back with her husband, and I had gone to spend a few days with Pastor and Mrs. John following the convention. Pastor Percy helped me to draft a letter and encouraged me to send it, though how grateful I was that he had counselled me not to tell others until things were more definite. I had a reply; the field would be New Guinea but they would have to check up with our own church council before I was accepted.

Tragically, Percy, who had just recovered from a severe breakdown, died. I heard no more from Australia. It seemed that the letter was never dealt with. How glad I was that I had not told my parents.

I have to admit that I was relieved. New Guinea, now Papua New Guinea! It was the uttermost part of the earth as far as I was concerned. Maybe God had again just been asking my willingness. I had never put Ireland entirely out of my mind. Besides, my father was suffering from senile dementia, as they called it in those days. I was needed at home.

I could have left home years ago. I realised that when I crossed swords with my father, as so easily happened that I was making life increasingly hard for my mother.

'Lord, make me a blessing at home, or I must go.' It seemed an impossibility to me, but God did it. My mother used to long for me to come home and regale them with all the humourous stories of the day, and bring some fresh air into her increasingly trying situation, and as she shared her trials with me I would help her to laugh about them.

Now, in this time of waiting, my father died and I was able to support my mother through her time of grief until she regained her health. I am so thankful that in the months that he was in Claybury, a psychiatric hospital near our home, in all his confusion I found Daddy gentle and sweet and it was such a comfort that I was able to hold his hand.

I had passed my driving test not so long before and now In this time was able to gain a certain confidence in driving. I also had promotion in teaching.

I would never have considered it before, not only because of my missionary call but because I felt that I had enough to do in coping with the responsibilities of my own class without taking on anything extra.

Now I read an advert for a deputy headmistress and it was as if a shaft of light was on it. Everyone encouraged me and I found myself deputy head of an Infants school in Forest Gate. Others had found the head, Miss Rolfe, difficult, but she thought the world of me and the eighteen months I was with her did so much to develop my confidence.

'Of course you must go on for a head-ship,' one of the inspectors told me, 'You are just what we're looking for.'

'But what about my missionary call? Lord, won't you speak to me about it?' That morning, driving to school, I saw an almond tree in blossom, and God's word to Jeremiah came to me, 'I am watching over my word to perform it.'

Shortly after I had a letter asking me to go as a teacher to Laiagam, in the highlands of New Guinea. I went to lie on the bed. I felt as if all the strength had drained out of me.

I used to feel sorry for myself, thinking how hard it would be to leave everyone I knew and go to an unknown and difficult situation, until God had given me the verse, 'Rejoice in your going out,' and I began to realise what a privilege he was giving to me.

Now, gradually, the joy replaced the fear. I did awake twice from a nightmare, both times about spiders.

'What are you going to do when you get to New Guinea,' my mother asked. I had yelled because there was a spider in my room. I would be leaving in a day or two.

'Never you mind about New Guinea,' I told her. 'You get it out for me.'

I had dreaded telling Miss Rolfe as she had been so appreciative of having me, but she took it calmly. 'What a good job you told me today,' she replied. 'I must inform the office.' I learned later that she already knew that she was dying of cancer.

Mother and I had decided to have a special holiday before I left home and drove together to see the Lake District and visit Joy who was working in the Wirral. We stopped to see the Falls of Ladore, tumbling and splashing, overcoming every obstacle in its joyful downward rushing. What a picture of the purposes of God, overcoming every rock of opposition. Then we went to another spectacular waterfall.

I stood on a bridge spanning the river and looked down on a drop of hundreds of feet to where the water crashed onto the rocks below. I have never liked heights and could not stand there.

'Lord,' I cried, 'that is what it feels like to me. I am taking a great leap of faith into the unknown, and I am afraid.'

Then deep in my heart, God answered me. 'But the river is not afraid.' It was true. The river had one purpose, to reach the sea. It rushed joyfully on its way. Then I recalled another word.

I had given up my lunch one day and had been walking the back streets of Hoxton, asking God to show me where he wanted me to go to answer his call. That evening a word came that I knew was for me.

'Your calling is not to a person or to a place. It is a joyful abandonment to your God.'

That was it. The river knew that joyful abandonment, and that is what I must prove too.

As I have said, we were in a church where God spoke through prophecy. When the letter came asking me to go to Laiagam as a teacher, I had shared only with my pastor. Of course I must go, but I longed for a word of confirmation and I wanted it from someone who knew nothing of my situation.

That Sunday, for the first time, John Langford, a prophet, was in our service. A word came through him, to 'one in particular, I will direct your paths.' I knew that I was that one and that I must step out in faith.

A farewell service was arranged. Surely here there would be some special word for me. But no, I had to go in faith.

I went up to Australia House, as I would be flying to Australia first as an emigrant. I gasped as the lift took off as soon as I stepped inside.

'Where are you going?' someone asked. 'New Guinea,' was my reply. I realised afterwards that she meant which floor did I want. She laughed. 'You didn't expect to take off straight away, did you.'

Now I was all packed up, waiting to hear of a flight. Suddenly I thought of what it would be like, leaving everyone and everything I knew, and stepping through the airport doors when my flight was called. 'Lord, I won't be able to do it.'

Then the Lord showed me, in a picture, of him going ahead of me. He told me, 'I am going. You can come with me or you can leave me.'

That is how it was. I quote from my diary. '3rd. August '67. It was a beautiful Summers day as Mother, with Mary, drove me right through the City, along the Embankment and past the Houses of Parliament and then out to Heathrow. Esther, home on furlough, was already there, with her parents, and helped me through with my luggage. The Holdens arrived, with Edith, and then the Ilford folk, with May, who had come all the way from Hereford, and a childhood friend, Joan. But where were the Spurdles? (He was now the Ilford pastor) At last they came, Mrs. Bush, our oldest member, with them.

Jim Holden prayed, and we sang 'Jesus is the joy of living.' I heard the call over the intercom. There were those terrible last embraces but I knew the Lord had already gone through those doors and I could not leave him. I walked through and there was no way back.

I felt desolate, so alone, - but only for a moment. My name was called and I was handed a box of chocolates and two lovely red roses. Dear Wendy and David had arrived late and sent them through to me. It saved my life. No more time to be sorry for myself. We were boarding the bus. One last wave to my dear family and then I was on the plane, flying to the other side of the world.

Joyful Abandonment

A brief stop at Istanbul. I was glad enough to have a wash. We seemed to be greeting a new day before we had left the night. I was unable to sleep. There were some lines of a poem pulsing through my head, something about 'above the funnels roaring and the fitful winds deploring, I could hear the cabin snoring with universal nose,' but I didn't hear any snoring. Probably no one else was able to sleep either, but no one stirred.

It was strange, feeling that the whole of the world was below us. Were those twinkling lights in Persia? or was it Pakistan? The stars were so bright, but as the sky lightened there was the new moon with the old moon in her arms and then the sun rose from beneath us, spreading vistas of glory between layers of clouds. I was on the wings of the morning.

A break again in Bombay. As the steam was rising from the tarmac after a sudden storm I was thinking of the McCulloughs, and Pastor Les Davies (now my brother in law) and his wife, newly arrived. We had visited them when I was on holiday with the Johns. Pastor and Mrs Copp were there too. Now he was in heaven, having died on the way back from Ghana, and we were now in the far places of the earth.

'I don't know what you are going to do in New Guinea. You need looking after.' It was Mary Smith, sitting next to me. A young woman, she was going out to join her fiance. I had a nose bleed, needed travel sickness tablets, and got into various predicaments, but I supposed the Lord would look after me in New Guinea, as he was then.

A stop at Singapore, and then Darwin. Australia at last, but still we had to fly for hours over the desert until eventually we saw the wide blue bay and had landed at Melbourne where Pastor Tate met me. He drove me out to Hawthorne, where I was to stay with Pastor and Mrs.McCabe.'

Pastor Joshua and his dear Chrissie had come from the home land many years before. He was away on a visit to Jigalong, our outreach to the Aborigines, when I arrived, but was soon back to help me in all that had to be done before the next lap of my journey in a months time.

'Hello Pauline.' I couldn't believe my eyes. I had gone to church with Mrs. McCabe, thinking I knew no one, and here was a friend from home. I had known that Lily had come to Australia, but to be here in Melbourne. How good God was.

The folk in the Punt Road church took me to their hearts and helped me in so many ways and the McCabes became my Australian Mum and Dad, but I was overawed by the vast distances around me. I had already come such a long way, but it was nothing here to speak of a thousand miles between one city and another, and there was still a great journey to be made before I would reach home. Yes, it had to be home for I had pulled up my roots. I had no where else to go.

'It isn't frightening is it?' I had asked Mary. I was remembering a holiday with her when she lived in Devon. Esther was abroad now so my holidays would not be quite so adventuresome - I had thought.

Trusting, I had set off with her, the path getting gradually steeper until suddenly I felt as if I was clinging on by my teeth, with the sea and rocks far below and the top of the cliff still way above.

'I can't go on,' I had declared, but it was too late, for the way back was far more frightening. Eventually she had coaxed me to the top.

I recalled this incident now as I faced the journey from Australia on into the highlands of New Guinea.

'Lord, I feel like I did when I was on the cliff path. I can't face the journey back and I haven't the courage to go on.' What was I to do?

Joyful Abandonment

CHAPTER THIRTEEN—THE ENDS OF THE EARTH

'You are facing vast distances, but I have pledged myself to come with you, and I want you to face your journey with confidence and joy.'

Confidence and joy? If it had been anyone else I would have said, It's all very well for you to talk, but it was the Lord speaking.

Yes, I had so longed for a prophetic word before I left U.K. but now, when I did not expect it, it came.

We had bought all my household goods, and prepacked furniture while I was in Melbourne, to be sent up by sea. I had spoken around the churches so that the folk would know this missionary who was being sent under their auspices. I had at last been interviewed by the missionary committee. Too bad if they didn't like me now.

It was a nice surprise to be told that my salary would be eight pounds a week. Pastor Tate had put 'a month' in his letter, and I had been prepared to believe that somehow the Lord would undertake. We had a laugh over that.

Now there was a special farewell service for me, and the Lord was speaking to me by name. There were other promises too, of the difficulties that I would face but that I would be able to turn to the Lord, readily and easily at all times, as to a friend who is alongside. More than thirty years later, those words are still so precious to me.

I stood now on the railway station when Ruth, the women's leader, breezed up with a box of chocolates and some magazines. 'Forget about the church and enjoy yourself,' she told me. Enjoy myself? I had always hated travelling, and especially alone, but wonderfully, I did enjoy these journeys. God was giving me confidence and joy.

A weekend in Sydney with Pastor and Mrs Hawkins. I Remember Nancy, his second wife, ,and I eating alone. Her Husband was glued to the television, watching his son, a racing driver, take part in this big race. What agony for his father. Paul was eventually killed in one such race. They advised me to book a sleeper for the overnight journey From there to Brisbane. I have never forgotten the beauty as I awoke to find the train chugging up through circuitous paths into the beautiful wooded hills. Pastor and Mrs Corr met me and were delighted that I had had a good nights sleep so that they could take me to the Lone Pine Sanctuary. I have a photo of me holding a koala bear to prove it, and of course there were kangaroos and wallabies.

As I leave them and fly over the coral seas and Great Barrier Reef towards Papua first, and then New Guinea, perhaps here I should pause to tell you a little of what lay before me.

Papua and New Guinea were still separate territories at that time, though all under the Australian government. Port Moresby and the coastal areas had known civilisation for many years, but the interior was so mountainous that many of its inhabitants had not had any contact with the outside world. Pastor Reah had come to UK back in 1955, just before we came into the church, telling of how they had gone in to make contact with these stone age people, living off their gardens and with no knowledge of civilisation. Missionaries were not allowed in to a territory until the government first went in and declared it safe. They recorded the names of the people in a village book. Once their names were given it seems that they knew that they were under authority.

Laiagam, where I was going, had only been opened up ten years ago, and while I was there we sometimes heard of new tribes that had been contacted, still living as cannibals. They had thought they were the only people in the world.

Some people question the work of missionaries, suggesting that it is better to leave people to their own ways and culture. However, once these people have been contacted, there is no way that they will be left as they were. They have got to enter into the twentieth century. Much of what they will learn will not be to their advantage; guns, tobacco and alcohol will soon be part of their way of life. They will enter our age of commercialism; and warfare, of which they already know plenty, will become far larger in scale, no longer fought with bows and arrows and fighting sticks.

They can't be left in their stone age existence, and so we too must go in and share with them that which has changed our lives, and given us courage to live in the twentieth century, the knowledge of God and of Jesus Christ his Son.

Wings of the Morning

And I was on my way, not because I loved these poor benighted heathen. How could I love them? I didn't know them, but God loved them and it was he who was sending me. I was going in simple obedience, because I loved him.

We landed in Port Moresby where I had my first sight of some 'natives', though we tried never to call them that. They were the nationals, the indigenous people.

The school children asked me if the Queen had natives working for her. I told them, 'Of course. People who are born in England are all natives of that country.'

These were clean and well dressed, working as porters in the airport, but I also saw a woman squatting on the ground, scantily clothed and feeding her baby.

I took a smaller plane now, with no air conditioning. It was a noisy, bumpy flight as we flew over mile after mile of high bush clad mountains scratched by hair like paths and coiling rivers.

Mount Hagen was a tiny airport but even so I missed the office and was wandering round one of the hangers. It was there that Laurie Darrington, the MAF pilot found me and took me on in his little yellow Cessna. I couldn't help thinking of the pilot who had been lost soon before I came up, his body never found. I had met his father while in Australia. He was a missionary too.

Our plane was loaded to near the safety limit, and the clouds, which can be death traps, were all around us, but Laurie was pointing out a village here, a mission station there and we were soon lining up to land on the air strip at Laiagam.

Never a good traveller, I was feeling green and deaf when I arrived. Here was a reception committee on the strip to welcome me. I don't think I made much of an impression for I heard later that there was a general agreement that I wouldn't last there more than a year.

Audrey, one of the nurses told me, 'You were such a lady when you arrived.' So I wasn't now? I agree I had not had any experience of roughing it. It was all I could do to manage to clamber into the back of the jeep and I certainly wasn't used to an outside toilet. But I stayed with John and Desma Hewitt for the first fortnight. They had a pleasant clap board house, with louvre glass in the windows and yes, indoor plumbing. No fear of spiders yet.

'I must get to the villages. I must get to the villages.' In my dream I had arrived to find Laiagam all brick buildings. I had dumped my suitcase and insisted on finding the villages. How ridiculous!

There weren't any brick buildings, though there was a store and an office and a handful of 'European' houses, but imagine my surprise when I arrived to find a football match in progress just as there had been in my dream.

I had seen pictures of these stone age people, but somehow I thought that already civilisation would have taken over. Instead I found a curious mixture of cultures; a man in a good pullover but only tankard leaves behind and a cloth in front for his lower covering; the younger women in their wrap around skirts and ample meri-blouses, which they could buy in the store, but many of the older women wore just a grass skirt which left their thighs uncovered. I was to find that in the villages they still lived off their gardens, as they had done through the centuries, but I had to get used to many more things before I would visit a village or go inside one of their houses.

Apart from teachers and nurses there were those running the stores programme, besides carpenters living on our mission station at Mamale, just a mile up the hill from the government station. There was supposed to be a house being built for me, but of far more importance was the new church which was under construction.

We were quite a gathering for the European service in the Hewitts lounge that evening. The girls had welcomed me with their hair in curlers in the afternoon, as they liked to dress up for this occasion. Apart from the Tilley lamp for lighting and the moths that fluttered around we could have been anywhere. For a moment I thought I was going to panic because of the moths but if everyone else was willing to endure them, why shouldn't I?

There was a Pastor Barnard speaking that night. He was a SDA missionary who flew his own plane and had had a miraculous escape when he was struck by the propeller. He and his wife were to become lovely friends.

There was so much to get used to. The missionaries spoke English with a liberal sprinkling of Pidgin, Enga and Aussie slang. John took me on a conducted tour of the mission in the morning. I didn't know if he was talking in Pidgin or Enga to the locals we met. I remember seeing people waiting for medicine. It was a leprosy clinic, though I saw no sign of them having the disease. Later on I saw people disfigured by it.

I had thought I might have had a day or two to get used to the place before I began work but that afternoon there was a teachers conference. I sat there feeling so lost and ignorant, but eventually found my tongue and began to ask questions, which is the only way to learn.

I was invited up to the 'lotu' (church) an old thatched building, with walls made from woven grass and open at the top for ventilation. It was my official welcome to the womens meeting. Most of them were washed and dressed and sat there so reverently. Many seemed old and wrinkled, even though they had babies at their breasts. I had a strange feeling that I had been there before, and I believe I had, in the missionary prayer meetings.

How can I describe the beauty of the tree clad mountains all around us? We were 6,000 feet up and the rarified air fresh and clean, though it left us breathless. The rain, which usually came after twelve o'clock, was torrential, and nights could be chilly.

'It's lovely over here, but the homesickness is terrible.' I had met British folk in Australia who told me this. And you have a husband and family, I thought. I remembered God's word, that Jesus bore our sicknesses and so I had claimed his protection from homesickness too. Wonderfully, now I felt that I had come home.

Soon after I arrived Dorothy gave us our first Enga lesson. Though there are at least 600 different languages, besides variations of dialect in the Territory, we were fortunate in that Enga was spoken throughout a wide area, and understood in some of the neighbouring tribes in the highlands.

'I counsel you to acquire a knowledge of the language in the place where you are going. Though you may not understand at the time, it will be of incalculable value in a time to come.'

This had been part of the word the Lord had spoken to me through Pastor Tate in my farewell service. It was years later that I was to understand why the Lord had said, 'in the place where you are going.'

It was soon after I came into the Apostolic Church that there was a word to the young people, in the Penygroes convention, that we should learn languages. Never good at languages at school I had now applied myself to German and made good progress. 'I think if you

83

were thrown in, you would swim,' a young German woman had told me.

'What good has that been now?' I was asked. It had been of great value. I had already acquired the discipline of language learning and when Dorothy was speaking about various tenses and parts of speech I was not out of my depth as some of the nurses were.

'You will need a language informant,' Dorothy told us. She had been our first missionary teacher and was fluent in Enga, while Philip her husband was compiling a dictionary. There had been no lesson books when she arrived. 'Try to spend an hour a day.'

I asked Rosa, Pastor Kopene's daughter to help me. The first day a quarter of an hour was all I could cope with, and the first time I tried to use what I had learned the people told me politely that they didn't speak English. But with God's command had been a gracious promise, that his help was assured.

I believe the greatest help the Lord gave me was joy in learning. I refused to use Pidgin, a language in itself, for it was only the men who had learned it, and my heart was overjoyed when I tried out a simple greeting to some women I met on the road.

'Oh,' they exclaimed, their delight evident, 'she talks the true talk.'

Some of my colleagues, especially the men, were younger and brighter and had a flair for languages. It was like the hare and the tortoise. I was determined to plod on, but would I ever be able to communicate? Could it be of 'inestimable value?'

MAF plane at Kopiango

CHAPTER FOURTEEN—THE VILLAGES

I was soon into the routine of life on the mission, the prayer meeting in the little office and then across to my own classroom where my boys would be hastily jumping into the ditch to slosh water over themselves. They got a black mark if they were not washed. There was so much mud and dirt there in the highlands.

Sometimes I would look at the selection of bows and arrows and axes dumped at the back of the classroom. I had to teach standard five, and some of my students had whiskers. We had to devise our own ways of learning how old the boys were, as it was only since the nurses came and kept records that anyone knew their age. I learned that if a child could not touch his ear by putting his hand over his head he was too young for school.

We didn't have many girls who went through to the senior classes. Girls were needed to work in the gardens, and if they stayed at school it meant separation from their parents who moved to different gardens at certain seasons. It was hard for them not to become wayward, with no parental restraint, and we felt there was some justification in the complaint that girls who went to school became prostitutes. However, we did have some girls who went through school, learning to walk with the Lord, and we thank God for them.

They were all supplied with a cloth, a laplap, which they wrapped around them, and they were given jumpers to wear in class, - not to be taken home or we would not see them again. They needed something for warmth since we did not have fires as they had in their houses. Some preferred their traditional covering of tankard leaves and at first I found it distasteful to see their naked thighs, but I soon became used to it, as to seeing the women clad in only a grass skirt.

The children were not expected to be clothed, though minimally, until they reached puberty, and some of the younger boys would revert to their naked state as soon as school was out. Even some babies, though, would be wearing a belt. This was ready to have a covering tucked into it.

Their basic diet was sweet potato, and at times the body odours would overwhelm me. Then I would fling open a window, put out my head and look at the mountains towering above us. 'As the mountains are round about Laiagam..' we used to say. If sometimes I thought of the possibility of a headship at home, with a little car and comfy flat, I would remind myself of how I had wept because of the burden of my missionary call and I knew I could not return.

We used to have the school children as helpers in our homes. I couldn't chop firewood, fetch water from the river when our tanks ran dry, or light a stove.

'Miss Thompson, please may I look at your pictures?' Little Popotada was never happier that when she had my box of old photos on the floor. She always knew which of the four children was me. She was a joy to have in the house, though we had to insist on certain standards of hygiene, and stealing was always a problem, as it had been with the little children of Hoxton. We used to say they had 'taking ways.'

Ill in bed with a high temperature, I had been dosed for malaria was so feeling terrible. When I struggled out of bed to find her stuffing her face with my chocolate biscuits I sent her packing. In retrospect I think I was very unwise. I deprived myself of a lovely friend and could surely have found some better remedy. I am sure that I, with her background, would have been tempted.

Prior to that I had needed a 'garden boy.'

'Why don't you try Akuni. He is a good worker.' I didn't think much of Ken's suggestion. I had found Akuni most disruptive in the classroom, but I agreed to give him a try. Soon he was helping in the house. He was wonderful, and used to organise the others when I went out on trek. A highly intelligent boy, his bad behaviour in class had been a cry for recognition. It was a lesson to me.

I was amused one day when a grubby gentleman with tankard leaves, and carrying a bow and arrows, took my hand and greeted me profusely as 'Akuni's mother.' Who was he? 'Oh, he is Akuni's father.' He was a very rich man, I was told, for he had many pigs.

Teaching was not hard, although the boys could be difficult. They loved to argue. With the cold wet weather much of their time was spent sitting round their fires, and arguing and story telling was the only art they knew. Then these older boys didn't see why they should have a woman to teach them when the Meehan boys were around. In their culture the men come first, then the pigs, women after that. But the lessons were not difficult. We had work books and radio programmes provided by the government, and the other teachers were so helpful. I lived for three months with Ken and Margaret Meehan, after a fortnight with the Hewitt family. It couldn't have been easy for newly weds to have a lodger, but they both came from big families and were great.

I was getting used to negotiating the muddy paths down to the school, to surviving when the mail plane did not get in, - we all lived for the mail, and at least I could understand the missionaries 'lingo', if not much Enga yet. But I was pressing on with my lessons. I had discovered by now that it was not just knowing the vocabulary, but using the right tone that was important.

'I don't know if there is much point in keeping my diary. Life is so quiet.' I promised never to say such a thing again. Everything happened that day.

The missing trusses for the new houses, which had caused so much frustration, had been found so off went Vern the carpenter with the tractor, only to slip a gear and end up in a ditch. Someone set out from Muriraga to rescue him but his motor bike broke down. Eventually the Meehan boys took the truck and found him nearly frozen from being out in the rain and the cold. Margaret meanwhile wanted to have a hot meal ready and the fire wouldn't burn. She helped it along with what she thought was paraffin and nearly had her head blown off and the house on fire. It had been white spirit.

'I nearly got cremated,' she told us, 'and I don't even believe in it.'

It was a great occasion when the new church had its official opening. Missionaries and friends gathered from all over the territory, and we had some wonderful meetings. It is easy to get dry spiritually when you are far from home and labouring in difficult circumstances, but these were times of refreshing, and I know that some who were ready to pack up their bags and leave found a willingness to stay and went on to do great things for the Lord.

The children from the other mission schools walked across the range for the occasion, and there was a lot of organising to do to feed them all and provide accommodation. We distinguished the true

Christians by those who were willing to take those from other tribes to share their homes.

We 'girls' were in teams to provide the meals. I was quite content to be a helper, thinking I would never have been able to organise cooking for such a crowd, but within a year we had another gathering of the clans and I cooked for thirty without turning a hair. It is wonderful how one's confidence grows.

'Ken! The hospital is on fire!' I stirred uneasily as someone thumped on the side of the transit house, but soon enough realised that this was no time to be in bed. People were shouting and we could hear this terrible roaring. The wooden hospital building was like an inferno.

It seemed that one of the Enga nurses had gone early to feed the babies and had panicked when the primus stove flared. Now an oxygen cylinder exploded and there was concern, not only for this building but for the rest of the mission. We formed a chain to pour buckets of water on the grass roof of the nurses houses close by.

Soon after the fire was out a strong wind blew up. How merciful was God that it had not happened before.

There was grief over the babies that had died, even though their expectation of life had been minimal, and with caring for the ones they saved we were all busy. One of our classrooms became a temporary clinic while the 'kalabus' (the prisoners) were sent up to put up another, near to the new houses that were being built.

'They have decided that it is better for the nurses to have the new houses and that you and Glenise should have the nurses houses.'

That was a blow. We had been looking forward to our new homes, but once I got adjusted to the idea I realised how good God was. Yes, our little houses had thatched roofs and no glass in the windows, and just one bed sitting room, but you could prop the window wide open and have a glorious view over the playground and across to the mountains. But meanwhile I had the transit house to myself for Ken and Margaret had moved in next door.

Though I was thirty six I had never lived on my own. If ever my parents were away I was unwell, a combination of being nervous and not bothering to cook I think, so I used to go and stay with my sister. How would I cope now?

After the initial shock I enjoyed unpacking my own possessions and making this ramshackle, tumble down old house a home. I pegged bright picture tea cloths into the walls made of woven grass, and spread some rugs on the floor.

The mission organ had been left there and this saved my life, being able to have a sing and a play. There was always someone passing, for the house was right beside the main path, and they would put their heads in my open window and greet me, but most of all I found that the Lord was real and near and I did not feel alone.

One evening I had been writing a letter to the missionary secretary, telling him of my joy, but that night I lay in my bed, shaking with fear because of the rustling and chattering of the rats. My joy had fled, until I realised, when Ken had been there I wasn't afraid. Why should I be now? Wasn't the Lord with me? He was far more capable that any man. I pulled my bed into the middle of the room, tucked up my covers and went to sleep. Not long after that I was given a kitten who was a wonderful ratter, and also a friend. She would always respond with a prrr when I spoke to her, and I wasn't bothered by rats after that.

Later on Jean gave me a lovely puppy who was always with me, so I was guarded from rats when I was on trek too, and pigs too.

On the mission field, it isn't the great dangers that trouble you as much as the little ones. 'Back to the flea pit,' Philip would call at the end of playtime. I soon learned that this was not just a figure of speech.

Fleas and house flies were always with us. You could rarely drink a cup of tea without at least one fly diving into it. The 'New Guinea wog,' gastro-enteritis was doubtless because of this. It hit us all from time to time. Then with living in such a close community if one person was upset it affected others, and there could be friction. And now I found that I was not enjoying my teaching. What was wrong?

Of course, I had always felt my niche was with the little ones, but here I had to have the older children who could already speak English. I understood that, but I believed the Lord wanted me to have joy in his service. Hadn't he promised me joy?

When I needed to be alone I would walk down towards the government station. There was a covered bridge over the Lagaip, and I would stand there and listen to the song of the river, and come back strengthened. Now I poured out my complaint. Then God showed me that my main work was not the teaching, but that I was to go out to the villages. But how could I? What was I to do? I didn't know, but once I accepted that this was to be my work somehow the Lord restored my joy and it wasn't too long before I was able to pass on my argumentative boys and had a younger class.

'Thompson-o! Thompson-o! Panda silyamo!' I was at Murip, with a class of new receptions. I had enough of the language now to cope. I had fifty children already and was explaining that I had no more room, but the little ones were shifting up to tell me, 'Look, here is room.'

It was government policy to teach only in English. I remember to my shame that we used to punish the older boys for speaking Enga in class, for school was the only opportunity they had to practice English, but with these new entrants I would say it in English, repeat it in Enga, and then say it in English again. It was wonderful how quickly we learned, and we had a happy relationship because I understood their language, - well, some of it.

'Do you want some ....' Tundi asked me, in Enga. 'What is it?' I asked. 'Shall I show you?' An hour later he returned with some sand from the river. I was learning. But back to those first months in Laiagam.

While the carpenters were busy erecting the church and the nurses houses, the Meehan boys who were jack of all trades, were busy building a house for Mukiwana, now known as Hannah, soon returning from high school to be our first indigenous teacher.

Our children were a first generation to have any education, and it was a great thing when their standard six students passed their exams and went to a mission high school on the coast. It was hard for them to be in a tropical climate, with different food and languages as well as customs and culture. Many from other missions had not stood as Christians but we were proud and happy that our three returned strong in the Lord.

I had been to visit some of our outlying churches with Ken and Margaret. They used to laugh at the way God always sent someone to help me when I came to creeks and gullies where I needed a hand. The Enga for 'give me your hand' was one of the first expressions I learned to recognise, while 'go outside and clean your nose,' was one of the first that I learned to say to the school children. They hadn't been brought up to use handkerchiefs.

'We went a much easier way this time,' I told Ken, having returned from Latalama, at the top of one of the mountains.

'Was the way easier, or is it you that have changed?' he asked. Well, maybe, for God had met with me.

Going on ahead one day, I again found myself in a predicament where I couldn't go on and couldn't go back. As I sat, shaking with fear, I felt the Lord telling me, 'I can't help cowards. It is only in the going that I can strengthen you.' Yes, God was changing me.

I was never lonely in my tumble down house. I was often down helping the nurses or would ask them up for a meal. I enjoyed entertaining. And now the standard six boys, and Hannah, began to call in the evenings. I knew that they came because they liked to cook their sweet potatoes in my oven, but still I enjoyed the company. Their English was excellent and it was a lovely opportunity to get to know them.

'The people in our villages would be very happy if you would visit them.' With the boys and Hannah as able companions and interpreters I was delighted to respond. The work in the villages was beginning. At first they had to help me over the stiles and through the bogs, and once one of them gave me a piggy back, and was not willing to put me down because it was quicker this way, but I soon grew stronger and less dependent.

Christmas in the tropics is different, but no, I didn't long for home, for my last Christmas had been a sad occasion. We had thought that we were all to have been together, but it hadn't worked out. Now I was glad to be where I knew God had sent me. I cooked a chicken dinner, successfully stuffing it 'out of my head' as I didn't have a recipe. This was for the single girls, 'unclaimed treasures' we used to call ourselves, and Ruth Cole had us all for tea, and we had had a joyful service in the church with all the folk from the outstations coming in.

Christmas was the long holiday, when everything closed down, but I was busy, and making great strides with my language learning. Then a young missionary from the coast came up to the highlands for a holiday. Suddenly I didn't know if I was on my head or my heels.

CHAPTER FIFTEEN—THE PLACE OF THE ASHES

We had several single young men on the mission field. There had been three passing through that weekend, but I was busy and did not even see Stan Chong, an eligible bachelor who worked in Wewak.

Then we were invited to a fellowship evening. I had been out on trek on my birthday, and had thought that no one would even have known about it, but imagine my surprise to find that it was a party for me, and there was a special gift, for it was there that I met John.

I have mentioned the prophetic picture the Lord had given me years ago. I was walking toward the Lord and someone had come so that our paths were parallel and we walked together into the glory. Because of this and other words, I had been believing for a husband.

Not so long before I had come out I was visiting the Knights where I met this German, young and handsome and gifted in evangelism. I had already been learning his language and there was a mutual attraction. It all seemed so right.

'Lord, all I want to know is if it is your will.'

'It will come to pass. You will walk together. You will walk in paths of suffering and bring sheaves to me.'

The word had seemed so clear and plain, spoken into my heart. How could I have imagined it? Yet it did not come to pass. We met a couple of times. After a wonderful day together at Kew Gardens he had given me cause to hope but then I heard no more.

Back in Manor Park, I was pinning pictures to my classroom wall, feeling desolate and rejected when it was as if the Lord came and put his arm around me to comfort me. 'Lord,' I told him, 'if I have you I can go through anything.' I wondered whether the child who was sitting there was aware of the wonderful presence of God as I was? I had known that there was no hope, but even so, it had been with pain that, soon after my arrival in New Guinea, I had heard that my German was now married.

John came to the highlands for a break from the humidity of the coast where he was working with the AOG mission and we had fallen in love.

Perhaps I had not understood. Was this word that I had hidden in my heart concerning him? With John from New Zealand and me from England, everyone seemed to think it a fairy tale romance. My pre- packed, DIY furniture had arrived not long before and I had been waiting, with longing, for someone to put it together for me. Now the Lord had sent me my very own carpenter.

'Look! A fire! Oh John, it must be the store!' We were out on John's motorbike when we saw the smoke and then the flames licking upward. We rushed back and John climbed right into the tank to pass out buckets of water but it could not be saved. It was another terrible tragedy. David and Betty lost all their possessions and could have lost their baby but for the bravery of one of the school boys. But when John was asked to stay on to help with building extra rooms to house them we were delighted that we would have more time together. It all seemed so right.

We had the little mission organ in my home. John would harmonise in his rich tenor while I sang and played. Then we would relax in front of the stove and listen to Beethoven on my portable record player. We had so much in common.

After three weeks together he returned to the coast. At first the letters and parcels were coming thick and fast. John sent me some spiked walking shoes which gave me 'hinds feet' when out on trek, but then there were long gaps and I knew it was not just because of the mail plane. In the end I was ill in bed with a broken heart.

'The place of the ashes.' Pastor Corr had preached on this, and now I was to prove that out of death comes new life.

A tune was haunting me, and Margaret was able to tell me the words,

'Some through deep waters, but God gives a song.' I must not look to the future, just take each day as it comes. I began to find a fresh joy in my work, and in fellowship with the nationals, and I suppose they realised that I needed them. But let me tell you how the Lord brought healing.

'If only I could see John once more, maybe I could get over it.' But how was that possible?

The Place of the Ashes

Frank and Ruth Carter invited me to Kopiago and it was agreed I was in need of a holiday. Hannah was to come with me and stay with Gwenda, but to get there we had to fly via Wewak and overnight there. In Stan Chong's store, who should I see but John? He too was in on a chance visit.

He had not seen us and I did not have the courage to approach him, but then I realised that if I didn't I would regret it for the rest of my life. Early next morning I went over to where he was staying and we spoke briefly. But our planes did not fly because of the weather. God was giving us longer together.

We walked along the sands, with the Pacific gently breaking on the shore, and the palm trees waving in a graceful back drop. An evening together with friends and then it was our last goodbye. We were very fond of each other, but our way was not together. I held his hand to my cheek in a last farewell and went inside.

'I will never forget this happy, happy time.' It was a dream that had comforted me when I realised that I was not going to hear from my German again. We had been on a journey, and then we got separated and there was all confusion, but as I woke I had been dreaming that I was pressing his hand to my cheek and saying these words. Now it was reality. In all the pain I knew that God had foreseen it and that this brief relationship had been God's gift to me, even though it had not led on to marriage.

'Maybe God has someone else for you.' It was one of the MAF pilot's wives giving us hospitality who was trying to comfort me, but I was thirty seven. Soon I would be too old to have a family. Maybe it was lack of faith, but I felt that I had to accept my life as a single woman.

It was while I was sitting above the lake at Kopiago that the Lord showed me the work that he had for me, of training the nationals in Sunday School and literacy work. It seemed so impossible that I could take on this task, but in a wonderful way now the Lord began to work things out.

'Where is your husband?' one of the dear women at Pipitaka was asking me? Had she remembered that I had visited there with John? I don't know, but I told her I had none. 'It is because of our children, isn't it.' To these people it did not matter that you did not have a husband, but not to have children!! You were not really a woman without a child, and yet they understood.

It was at Kurap that I heard the women talking about the 'Little children's mother.' I was sure they were referring to Miriam for she was mother of six, but no. I often heard them say it when she was not around. There was no doubt about it. This was what they called me. If I had had my own husband and family I could not have been 'Wane Kole Endagi' the Little Children's Mother. Looking back it is easy to see the Lord's purposes, but it isn't easy to understand at the time and healing comes slowly.

Friday afternoon was our staff prayer meeting. We listened to a tape that Ken's brother Rex had sent. He spoke on Jesus being the apostle and high priest of our confession, of the importance of making a good confession. If we are grumbling and asking why, Jesus has nothing to present to the Father, but if we will bring his own word to him, he cannot deny us.

I went back home, knelt by my bed and prayed, 'Lord, I am delighting myself in you and you are giving me the desires of my heart.' The earth didn't shake. I didn't know then that it was a turning point, but from then on I had a joy and peace and wouldn't have been anywhere else in the world.

I was still living in the transit house, with thatch that the rain poured through after a few days dry, a floor that was rotten and sometimes a leg of your chair would go through, tipping you onto the floor, and what was that bulge in the ceiling that moved if your prodded it? We never did find out. My 'little crooked house,' John called it. But it was here that I was reading the story of Ruth and I told the Lord, I feel just as she did. These people are my people. I want to live and die with them.

Margaret used to be responsible for the Sunday School work. The teachers would gather and she would tell them the story, and they would write out the text in Enga to take back to their villages. I used to help Margaret, filled in for her when she had hepatitis, and when she started a family I took over. The teachers were mostly of our school children, though there were one or two of the nurses too.

The lessons were from a syllabus prepared in Australia, but in wonderful ways they would be timed to meet a present need. I believe in systematic Bible study.

There was the time when some of our Christians were going to the singsing. Were we wrong in expecting a strong line of demarcation between us and the world? The lesson that week was about David going to Achish for refuge and finding that he was fighting on the wrong side.

Then there was the time I was visiting the Sunday School at Tilya. The vine bridge swung and swayed as I crossed the turbulent waters, and the foot and hand holds seemed to be getting less and less. I had a panic attack. Eventually reaching the other side I determined I was not going back over the bridge but I was told that there was no other way. I continued on my journey, up the mountain as usual, and tried not to think about the bridge. The children were repeating the text they had learned the previous week.

'I will trust and not be afraid.' I told the children how afraid I had been, but that now I was going to trust. When we got to the river I spoke out God's word, and somehow I had the sense to take off my shoes too. That made it easier to grip on the branches. When we were safely back on our side Hannah and I sat and laughed because our fear had gone. I crossed many vine and log bridges after that, but only if there was a Sunday School at the other side. I wouldn't do it for pleasure.

'I would like to go and spend a weekend in these outstations and take a series of meetings.' I couldn't understand why Pastor Hewitt was not more enthusiastic when I asked his permission but when I was returning from a visit to a toilet hole in the dark and mud and wet and finding the house they had given me to sleep in overrun by cockroaches, I understood that I had had to do it because of my own conviction.

Pastor Kopene came to visit me to tell me that I had the blessing of the elders to 'go out into the villages.' That was the words Hannah used as she interpreted. I was thrilled for it was the word God had spoken to me all those years before.

'These people love stories about their gardens,' Philip told me. Their lives centred round their gardens and their pigs. So I made up a story, based on the Sower, about an Enga boy and how he first heard the gospel. The school boys drew the pictures and I cut them out to make a flannelgraph. As far as we knew there was no art in the culture of these mountain people, yet the boys make wonderful pictures.

'That is a story about us,' some of the women told Hannah. My novel, The Broken Bow, came out of this. Then I used Esther's story about Samuel's body house. It was beautiful on the outside but inside it was dark and full of rubbish. He had to learn to ask Jesus into his house. The wooden box that we had painted to represent Samuel's house was very useful for carrying my supplies. And they loved my little puppet that I had made, who helped me to tell the story of the wordless book. I had a projector and a motor bike battery and showed some slides of the people themselves before my film strips of a Bible story. Some of the school boys would cheerfully shoulder my loads. 'We are helping you to do God's work,' they would say.

Thirty years later, one of these boys has written an account Of these trips and the impact the stories had on his life. At first I had Hannah always with me. She was my 'shepherd' the people said, and a capable interpreter.

Our first weekend was at Kepelam. There was a road, and a disused mission house there, so I was starting off the easy way. In other places the people usually gave me the use of a 'European style' house. Theirs were low and dark, but these still had to have a fire in the centre, and no chimney because that would make the house cold. I thought I had something in my eye the morning after one such weekend, but the pain was caused through sitting in the smoke. I had to learn to keep out of it.

Then there was the problem of toilets. Sometimes there was some semblance of a toilet house, though on one occasion I was shown a hole, with no privacy. I was told that they were going to build the house on Monday. I could not wait two days, but I had to wait until it was dark. I was touched when on one occasion I was told that one of the school boys had set too and dug a hole and made some sort of shelter for me. They cared for us, if they did think we had strange ways.

'You be careful,' one of the nurses cautioned as I was setting out on trek. 'There are spiders that lurk in toilet holes. We have people come with very bad bites.'

I don't know to this day whether she was deliberately trying to scare me. I learned that there were spiders, looking quite harmless that could give a bad bite, but the wonderful thing is that they did not scare me. God had delivered me from this fear, and I knew I could trust him to protect me.

Hannah was only with me for a few weeks. She married Masikili and returned with him for further training. The next standard six boys, who had all passed their exams with flying colours, had gone too and I was dependant now on my class 5 boys for interpreters. They managed fine on every day subjects but when I spoke of repentance or other spiritual issues you could feel them fading away for they did not have a personal experience. God was giving me a push.

I had to prepare my messages in Enga, getting them checked of course, and then I read them. With telling the same stories over and over I became more fluent and eventually managed without my book.

I was working hard but longed to go to the Lutheran language school. No, they couldn't take in people from other missions, but they gave us a set of their tapes. God had promised me his help and now with these I began to make strides.

Val

But before then I had had a wonderful experience. Hannah had not been ready and so we had not set out early enough for our weekend to Yago. We had been caught in a tropical downpour. It was about an hour's trek for the young men, but took me nearer two. I had been soaked to the skin, and with the rats and fleas and smoke in the house where I slept I awoke the next morning feeling the worst for wear.

'Serves you right,' I told myself. 'You should get on with your teaching. You just wanted to do something different.' I came outside, where the sun was shining, the children playing happily, and went into the church. There I opened my Bible and read the words, 'the children God has given me.' They could have been in letters of gold. God had spoken. This was his work, and these were my children. This word is still very meaningful to me.

Ruth Cole, one of the nurses, had left us now and Valerie came to take her place. What a joy to have someone from England. We had not met before but we had many mutual acquaintances and she was like a breath of fresh air.

'Will she have an accent like you?' Margaret asked, as we went to the air strip to welcome her.

'I'm not the one with an accent. It is you lot who have the accent,' I replied. I was joking, and yet in my heart I had really thought that this was so. In speaking of it, I realised how ridiculous I was.

Then Lily came up for a Christmas holiday. How good God was. He was working out his purposes. Everything was going well. Little did I know of the sword of Damocles that was waiting to fall.

Ken and Margaret Meehan and Kevin

CHAPTER SIXTEEN—TO THE ENDS OF THE EARTH

'We are willing to pay your fare home.'

I had been accepted by the Missionary Board on the condition that I did nine years before they would pay my fare back to England. After a year they had told me that I could take my furlough in UK, that would be after four years. I suppose they had been testing me. But now I had been there less than two years and we heard that our stores, medical and teaching programmes were all to be closed. We had known that we were working ourselves out of a job, and that eventually the nationals would take over, but to be cut off like that! It was a bomb shell.

How could I return to UK? This was my home, these people my people. The alternative was to work with the government, but that meant I could be sent anywhere in the Territory. Pay would have been much better and I could have afforded my own transport, but it was doubtful whether I would have been able to continue with the Sunday School work.

Then there was a ray of hope, the possibility of my working with the New Zealand board, over the range. Ken and Margaret had already been transferred there. At last I had an official letter, offering me to join their staff.

'Lord, all I want to know is your will.' I believed the Lord had answered me. 'This is my will.'

I wrote off, accepting. Then it seemed that all hell was let loose. Before, there had been no guarantee that I could teach at the government school at Laiagam, but now I was told that I would be letting everyone down and bringing our mission into disrepute if I did not stay on there.

I felt that our missionary board cared nothing for God's will in my life and that they were willing to 'throw me to the wolves' for the sake of their good name.

I was visiting Philip and Dorothy when they read the letter to me. In a deep depression I came home, knelt by my bed. 'Lord, you have got to help me,' I cried.

I did not expect help to come in the way it did. I read the words of David, 'Fret not yourself in any wise to do evil.' God was telling me, never mind what you think others are doing wrong. You are doing wrong by fretting about it. Leave it with me.

He gave me grace to do this.

Many of our family at Laiagam were leaving. Valerie had been asked to replace Gwenda in the clinic work at Lake Kopiago and was soon on her way. Government people began to move into the empty mission houses. I had a bachelor living next door to me, managing the store which had been taken over by Waso. The Hewitt family left and the Stephensons with their adopted baby Joel came as superintendent.

I had a lovely Christmas holiday with Val and the Jourdains at Kopiago. At 4,000 feet the climate was ideal. The lake, with its floating islands, was like a jewel among the mountains. Often, if Val was busy, I would laze on an air bed or on the raft, and once a small boy took me out to an island in his dug out canoe. Sometimes I accompanied Val on her clinics and helped with her Sunday School work.

Kopiago was a territory that had only been opened for about four years, and it was nothing to see men with bones in their noses. At the Christmas 'sing-sing' the men would be adorned with their impressive wigs, made from human hair, and wearing their war paint. They used the wonderful plumage of the birds of paradise by way of adornment.

On occasions we saw some of the Hewa people, who had been contacted more recently again, and it was a thrill to meet a young couple who, although they were dressed still in their scanty covering of leaves, had faces shining for they had come to know the God who had come to seek and save such as them.

Driving up the mountain tracks was even more dangerous than the road to Muriraga. Val gave me some chewing gum to help me overcome my nerves. It stuck to my false teeth. It certainly took my mind off the dangers of the road as I struggled to get unstuck.

Word had always gone out ahead, and there would be a crowd of mothers and babies waiting for her clinics.

One day Val had gathered the children to rehearse their Christmas play. 'Where is Mary, and Joseph?' 'Oh, they have gone to the market.' But the Nativity play on Christmas morning, a lolly scramble after, and then the Jourdain boys flying the kites they had received was a precious memory.

My holiday was nearly over. It was New Year's Eve. We were invited to a party run by the local Government officer. I felt like a fish our of water, and again a terrible depression overcame me. I was supposed to be moving to Kurap, a remote mission station on the New Zealand side, sharing the teaching with Jean Rosie, but as yet there was no house for me. I had already been told that the only man who would be on our station did not agree with single missionaries being in such a situation. I certainly didn't think it ideal, but what was I to do about it? And how would I survive having to share a home in cramped conditions? If only I would learn not to try to look into the future. In the end I could have had two houses for myself.

'We are going to provide motor bikes so that at least you and Jean will have your own transport.'

Yes, the Purdie family were unable to return from their furlough in New Zealand so instead of coming up to Kurap the Cullen's must stay on the main station in Kandep. Jean and I would be on our own. The large family house, perched on the side of the mountain, would be all for me.

That I had my motor cycle licence had always seemed like a miracle to me. Back in 1954, or thereabouts, my brother John had asked me to accompany him on a tour of Germany to visit some groups of Bible Students and he wanted me to be able to help with the driving.

'How do I stop it?'

'You get it started first.' I was attempting to ride his BSA 350. True enough, it took me long enough to learn how to start. I did better on David's little Bantam and eventually applied for my test, but the date they gave me was too late for our trip.

I remember being ill in bed and terribly worried. Somehow it seemed all important that I must pass this test. Then I felt the Lord came to tell me, Stop looking at this problem. Just look to me.

Wonderfully they gave me an earlier date and I went off with the promise, 'I work and who can hinder it.' Yes, I had passed. But why? I only drove once in Germany. John's bike was too heavy for me. I bought myself a moped after that, thinking that I would easily cope with it, but I had a great burst of generosity, and offered it to the church. I was terrified of the thing. Pastor Blay was grateful to have it, and I more than thankful to go by public transport.

In Laiagam I had hired the mission bike on some occasions, but had never felt confident on it and preferred to walk with the school children who always had to accompany me to carry my loads.

But now at last I was to understand why I had had to go through all that trauma to pass my test. At last I would make friends with the bike. I drove on a practice run to collect the mail at the air strip. I did eventually get back safely. Then I was to drive up to Kurap. I managed all right on the flattish road and called in to Murip where Ken and Margaret were. On then past the Catholic mission station with the church with the outstanding murals that the local children had designed. Up now a further eight miles into the mountains. The road got steeper, the stones larger. The poor little bike roared and growled. At last my strength gave out. It couldn't hold it any longer.

What was I to do? I couldn't push it and I couldn't leave it there.

Before I called the answer came. Someone stepped out of the hedge and took the bike while I walked beside him up the last steep climb to the mission station. Where he had appeared from I had no idea. I only know that God was watching over me. I knew too I would rather live in isolation for the rest of my life than attempt to drive a bike again. This remains a mystery in my experience.

Jean, like Glenise, had had her twenty first birthday on the mission field. I admired these young girls so much for their courage. Now she and I had not only to cope with the school but with all the challenge of an isolated mission station on our own.

It was nothing to see children there with joints missing from their fingers. This was illegal now, of course, but people used to cut off a finger if someone 'gave them shame,' and a mother might punish her new born child if she had a difficult labour.

It was interesting to see the games these children played. They had their own version of marbles, using the fat acorns from their oak trees, and they played a game similar to our hopscotch. They used vines for skipping too.

We had contact with the other mission stations by radio but then there was the matter of keeping the batteries charged. My Pidgin was not up to much as I was concentrating on learning Enga, but Jean was fluent in Pidgin, and Ken was only twelve miles away.

He came up and helped us to sort out the new entrants and talked to the councillors and he and Margaret visited us as often as they could.

We had some excitement when Jean drove down to Kandep on the bike and met a young German who was the manager of the store there and they fell in love. We had lots of visits then and one Sunday morning they announced their engagement.

How did I feel? Envious? No, the Lord had healed my broken heart, and I remember I had so much joy in greeting the people as they gathered for church and practising my Enga on them that I felt that the joy of this young couple could not be greater than mine was. How good is our God.

It was not government policy that single girls should be in such an isolated situation, and when we called up over the sched to say that there was fighting up the valley and that they were carrying down the wounded you can imagine that there was some consternation. Dieter, Jean's fiance set out in a truck with some policemen and they came roaring on their way. They imagined us shut up in the mission house with men running round outside with bows and arrows, and it did nothing to calm them when they came to a bridge that was in need of repair and there was no way to proceed. But the fight had been far away from us and we were safe and unperturbed.

But Jean had battled against the loneliness and isolation for too long and at last she gave up. I packed her off on her bike to stay with the Cullens and heard over the sched that she was going home. So there was I, having been worried about the housing situation. Now I had two houses to myself.

I felt that I was at the ends of the earth, and yet I was not conscious of being lonely, or afraid, though I did lose weight at that time. I suppose there was tension, but I knew I had many friends around me. There was Kepa, one of our school children, who helped me in the house. He was not of the brightest, but had a lovely sense of humour and was so kind. His grandmother was one of the first Christians, still living in her stone age existence, but having a hunger for the word of God. When I read to her from the epistles of Paul, newly translated, I could not understand her excited talk, except, 'The light is shining.'

There was another occasion, when the Cullens were with us. Miriam told her interpreter to ask, Do they understand? 'When we are here, we understand,' one of the women replied, 'but when we go away, our minds are dark.' We sought to teach them to know the abiding presence of Jesus, the light of the world, and of course longed for them to be able to possess and read God's word.

It is around the stories of many of these Christians that I wrote The Broken Bow. Matthew's Mountain too was written from my experiences in Kurap, although it was based on the Payella airstrip, just opened, pointed out to me when I was flying to Kopiago.

I didn't find the teaching easy. These children were not disciplined at home. Their parents would laugh at their disobedience, until they lost their tempers and then they might throw a spade, or even a burning stick at them.

'Shoe-moko, shoe--moko' the children would whisper if they could see that my patience was growing thin. Yes, I would sometimes give them a wallop with my shoe, for a slap hurt me far more than them. They were used to going naked and their skins were tough. But I never lost my voice, as I used to when teaching in London. The children were not used to radio and television in the background. To them, every sound was of significance and if I spoke they were listening.

We tried to teach them to wear some clothing. I laughed when one child came to school with nothing but a shirt. I took if off and tied it round his waste as an apron, but he then was embarrassed because his buttocks were bare. It obviously didn't matter if he was completely naked.

We found a little organ that Pastor Reah, our first missionary, had brought up with him. I had a lovely Yamaha pedal organ that I had bought from the Stephens, in my home, so I took this one to school. The children loved it when I played and we all sang, and when I ran out of breath they would kneel and work the bellows for me.

Tuni was a little cripple boy on the compound. We learned eventually that his twisted limbs were caused through leprosy and he and his mother were sent to a hospital. If his father couldn't carry him to school they would push him down in the wheel barrow. I don't know if he learned anything else but he did learn that Jesus loved him. When we sang the choruses he would laugh and clap his hands, full of joy.

I continued visiting the outstations, trying to awaken the people to the need to teach their children. Some children had walked for an hour through mud and mire to come to school but were arriving late and were too tired to learn so I gave the worker instruction in how to teach them and he started an Enga school.

It was an adventure for me to get to their village, climbing mountains and wading through swamp. I needed a bucket of water to get the mud off my legs when I arrived, and by now I had learned the importance of asking for 'good' water for my kettle. Often on these journeys I would collapse, declaring I was dying, but I always managed to get up and go on again and always the joy of the Lord was my strength.

On one occasion the boys carried the message that Miss Thompson had broken her leg, but it was only the skin that was broken. I had a blister.

I wasn't on my own too long, and Ken had been coming up each morning, while Margaret taught his class, but this couldn't continue. There was news that the Purdies would be returning and so the Cullen family would be coming to Kurap but we were still in need of another teacher. Ken and Margaret were due for furlough. What was to be done?

'Didn't you say your sister might come up to visit you? Would you ask her if she would be willing to help out for a few months?' Mary had had a breakdown, and leaving her husband had returned home to my mother, not many months after I had left. Was it possible that she could make the long journey and face the hardships up here?

Jean's wedding

CHAPTER SEVENTEEN—TO TEACH OTHERS ALSO

The Cullen family with their five, soon six, children had come up to Kurap now. I had already moved into Jean's house.

'Sierra Delta, Sierra Delta.' The radio was on as it was time for 'School of the air.' A teacher at Mount Hagen gathered the children through the radio, to supplement their correspondence lessons which Miriam had to supervise. I loved it when it coincided with our coffee break.

Experienced missionaries, the Cullen's were right behind me in my language study and the Sunday School work.

We were on the border of Duna country. One day someone spoke in Duna.

'What did they say, Auntie Pauline?' asked Joyjoy.

'I don't understand their language.'

'You do. You know you do.' Someone had confidence in my ability. She hadn't realised they were different languages.

I not only spoke Enga to my house boy, but to my dog and cat. Jean had given me my puppy Dinky, short for 'adikipigi,' 'friend,' and then Dieter had brought up a poor neglected kitten that we called Pussy Pakiah, which also means 'friendly.' They ate out of the same dish and did everything together.

'Can Dinky speak Enga, Auntie Pauline?' Davey asked. Because the dog responded to my commands in Enga he thought she could speak it too.

I started to go down to the early morning prayer meeting with the local Christians. One morning I had such a blessing. Tongues were pouring out of me. From then on I was not well.

I have never resolved the question of whether the enemy attacks because we have had a blessing, or whether the Lord gives us a special blessing to prepare us for some trial that lies ahead.

'If you were older, I would have thought it was your heart,' Miriam told me. Oh no, not my heart again.

When I had been struggling in health following my previous experience, I had had a word from the Lord that 'I would rejoice, not

110

only spiritually but physically,' and it came true. I used to marvel at the way I climbed the mountains and survived these exhausting treks. Often I had the experience of physical rejoicing as I set out on an arduous journey.

'You. You are just a stick in the mud.' It was one of my class mates at high school that had made this scathing comment, - and it was probably true at that time, but I had often laughed about it when I found myself almost up to my knees in one of the many bogs I had to negotiate. But now it was all I could do to get down to the school.

They arranged for me to fly out to Mount Hagen to see a doctor. Wonderfully there was one of the best specialists from Australia in the territory at that time. 'With blood pressure like that you could live to be ninety,' he told me.

'I'm not worried about being ninety. I just want another ten years to fulfil my missionary call.' I didn't say it out loud of course, but God heard and granted. I was suffering from anaemia, caused through living at such a high altitude. I had the first of the very painful injections at the Laiagam hospital and Miriam was able to give me the rest up in Kurap.

'Pauline didn't die.' I only had a curtain for a bedroom door and three year old Danny had taken us by surprise. I was glad I 'didn't die', but Miriam explained that he was trying to say, 'didn't cry.'

Evelyn, the youngest of a family of musical missionaries had come up to help with the teaching. It was lovely to hear her sing with her ukelele. They were building another house for her. Then Jean came back for her wedding. That was a great occasion. I was one of the bridesmaids. So was my sister not needed now?

Mary had a conviction that it was God's will for her to come, but not until the new year, when Ken and Margaret would be on furlough. It was decided that mary and I should hold the fort at the mission station at Murip together, but once the Meehans returned we would have a teacher spare. We have a God who gives us the desire of our hearts. Mary was to be allowed to teach in my place while I gave myself to full time language study and the Sunday School work.

Kapusa, Philip we call him now, was to come across from Laiagam to work with me as my language informant. He had just failed to pass into high school and was bitterly disappointed but it must have been all in God's plan for the Lord opened a door for him after his time with us and he went on from there to university.

'Come on, no one can be that wonderful,' Margaret teased me, when I was bragging about my big sister. She had always been the one who could turn her hand to anything.

At last the day came. I had been to a New Guinea Keswick at Banz, a Bible college outside Hagen. It was a wonderful experience to meet missionaries from all over the territory. We were six of us in bunk beds and there was no privacy at all in the communal bathroom. I thought I was used to roughing it, but was so grateful when I palled up with Suzanne and she found a place for me where she was staying in one of the houses.

Now I was at the airport. At last the plane came in but where was Mary?

'Excuse me, but are you Auntie Pauline's sister or her friend?' We had been invited for a meal with the Cullen's and it was Delise who was asking. We have often laughed, and still send each other cards 'From your sister and friend.'

We had been so excited at the thought of being together but it was so long since we had seen each other and when Mary eventually emerged from the plane I hardly knew her. Of course, four years had gone by and Mary's health as well as her marriage had broken. It was wonderful that she had had the courage to face that journey alone, 'to the ends of the earth.'

I had always thought she could do things because she had more brains than me. Now I realised that more than anything it is a matter of confidence. With her unhappy experiences she had lost hers, and though we did not know it she had a brain tumour. I am sad that I was not as understanding as I should have been, but in it all it was wonderful to have her. Most of our missionaries had others of their families on the field, and now I had someone to stand with me.

We stayed a few days with Jean and Dieter, who were now living in Mount Hagen, until we could be flown in to Laiagam, and from there on we would go by truck.

'Whatever is happening?' We rushed to the window to see highlanders in their war paint, their spears in their hands and chanting aggressively as they ran along the road. Poor Mary must have found it terrifying. It seems they were demonstrating over some land dispute, and there were many such. When the Europeans had first arrived they had thought that it was all arranged that they were buying land, but these indigenous people would never have parted with that which belonged to their ancestors if they had understood.

Looking back, I marvel that there was no fear in my heart. These people were my friends. There was only one occasion when I did feel afraid and that was when I was staying near to a government station, and the men had been drinking. There was no drunkenness out in the villages.

Even after Mary arrived I still had occasions when I was on my own. We had all been in Murip for a last farewell for Ken and Margaret before they went back to New Zealand for a well earned furlough, as we called it. For some reason I had to hold the fort while Mary returned to Kurap with Evelyn. What a feeling of desolation as I watched the truck drive off. It was a large mission house. Pastor Torpe's house was within sight, and maybe call, if I could make my voice carry, but all around were wide open grass lands with the mountains away in the distance. I walked down to the bedroom wondering how I was to survive, when I found myself singing.

'Whisper a prayer in the morning..' only I wasn't singing it in English. The Lord was giving it to me in Enga. Suddenly I was aware of the sweetness of the presence of the Lord. Joy and peace. God was keeping his promise.

There was another occasion. We were in Kurap and Mary was taken ill. Ken came up and took her to the Lutheran mission station where they had agreed to look after her. I sent Evelyn to be with her on the ride down and she could not get transport back for a day or two, so again I was left, and the school and the radio sched to cope with, but God is wonderful.

One Sunday, the morning service was over and I returned to my house and shut the door. It was only one o'clock and for the rest of the day. I did have a battery run record player but that was my only form of entertainment. Suddenly I realised I was shutting the door on my friends. They were still sitting around talking and were so pleased when I made some pretext and went and sat with them on the grass, chatting with them as best I was able.

But at last the day came when I could give myself fully to language study and the children's work. Mary and Evelyn were ably coping with the teaching. We were part of the National Teaching service now and there was a high standard to maintain. Philip had arrived, and had the use of a house close by. He was to be my language informant.

While in Laiagam I had gone away for a week at a time to live in a village without an interpreter. It is the only way to learn, to make yourself speak the language. I tried to live as they did, but I could never fill my poor stomach with enough sweet potato to give me the nourishment I needed. We were warned never to eat pork unless we had cooked it ourselves, but when someone came from a pig feast and offered us some, I felt that nothing had tasted so good.

I would have liked to have spoken only Enga now, but it wouldn't have been fair to Mary, or Philip, as he wanted to improve his English, so we decided it would be Enga up until five o'clock and English after that.

'Oh dear, will five o'clock never come?' I would be struggling to express myself in Enga, longing to speak in my own language, but we are perverse creatures. By the time we were getting our meal I was in Enga mode and couldn't think in English.

I had a group of boys who came to my house for a literacy class. It is not difficult to learn to read a language recently reduced to writing as it is all phonetic and they soon went off with a copy of a gospel as a prize. Then I would take the occasional assembly. It was always interpreted for the little ones, so I did this too in Enga. On Friday I gave the lesson to the Sunday School teachers. I began to prepare lessons that I hoped might be used throughout the valley.

Then the call came, Come over to Muriraga and help us. I was thrilled.

We had had missionaries there for some years. The church would be full on a Sunday, but there was little sign of spiritual growth. At last it was decided to withdraw our expatriate staff. Pastor Arenda was sent to be in charge of the work.

'Pray! Please pray!' He was calling up on the radio, not to ask for material, but spiritual supplies. That dear faithful man of God wept and prayed and fasted and now God was moving by his spirit.

I had been to Muriraga when Brian and Carol Cole were there. I trekked out to outstations, climbed mountains, waded through bogs, crossed vine bridges that would look spectacular even in a Tarzan film and attended a funeral where they were still sitting around waiting for the man to die. He seemed happy to be sat up to have his photo taken. Alas, the film was spoiled and I have no record of this trip.

Even when I went to such effort the parents were not always concerned that their children should attend, but now things were very different.

'No, I'm sorry. There won't be room for the boys.' There was a lift for me in the landrover, but it looked as if I would have to go without an interpreter, for there wasn't room for Philip and he wasn't prepared to walk, not because of the distance but because it meant passing through other tribal territory.

He did turn up the next day, but it had given me a chance to know that I could survive on my own. I still couldn't keep up with a conversation around a room but I could talk to people one to one, where I could ask them to repeat what I had not understood.

What a wonderful week I had there; the fellowship in the home with the pastor and his wife was sweeet. It was rare to see a husband and wife living together in mutual respect as they were, though I was amused that when Arenda left he greeted everyone but his wife. This was their custom I suppose.

We had children's meetings every morning. They could come skipping over the mountains that I found so exhausting to climb, and because the parents had put their ways right, they saw that they came. The elders were there learning and after, I had sessions with them, giving them the biblical principles of children's work. The women too wanted to be included, and their meeting was given over to this.

I went with Pastor Arenda to visit the school, and wished I had been more prepared to speak to the children. I realised that this too was an important part of the children's ministry, and of the need to prepare a syllabus.

While there I sat in on a palaver. The people were discussing the possibility of independence. They decided, not yet, but of course the coastal people wanted it and it came soon after we left.

But now my heart was singing at the way my work was opening up. I expected to be returning to Kurap to teach, for my term of full time language study was over and Kapusa would be leaving us, but on reaching Laiagam I was told that Hannah and Masikili were already teaching there and would I stay on for a week to take children's meetings there?

How wonderfully everything was working out. We were so proud of these, our first school children, who had survived the tension of living between a stone age and twentieth century civilisation and, standing firm as Christians, were taking over our schools.

All that was needed now was the missionary board to agree for me to give myself full time to the work of training the nationals in the Sunday School work.

'If Mary were to work for the government she would be able to support you.' It was Dorothy and Phil who came up with this suggestion, and with a broken marriage Mary had no desire to stay in UK.

'Whatever happens, this work that you have done has not been in vain.' I felt that in some way Openakali, a faithful elder, was prophesying. I could only get the gist of what he was saying but afterwards I remembered and was comforted.

The Purdies visited us in Kurap. We were packing up now ready for our furlough. Stuart tried to prepare me that things might not go as I had hoped.

We were in Laiagam when he had the letter and had to tell me that the board could not see their way for me to return. As he was talking a beautiful rainbow framed the valley. How could I be discouraged? This was God's work. He had called me. His word had been coming to pass so wonderfully. Nothing could frustrate his purposes.

With Mary at Kurap

CHAPTER EIGHTEEN—HOME AGAIN

'You are thinking about going to your own home, but I am thinking about how I would like to go to high school.'

Philip was right. Enthusiastic, yes, and thrilled too as I was at the way the children's work was opening up, it was time to return to UK. Mary would have been with me a year and we were getting excited.

I had asked to delay my going as I had not wanted to endure an English winter, but now we were beginning to make plans.

Whatever the missionary board said, I was convinced that I would be coming back, and that this was my life's work. When we were invited to a ladies weekend with the Lutherans and there was not room for us all on the plane, I was happy to be left behind, sure that I would have other opportunities.

In my heart I had wondered how I was going to find the strength to go on these strenuous treks for the rest of my life. There was the time when the rain began to pour through the roof of my temporary shelter. A highland warrior, dressed in tankard leaves, produced an umbrella and escorted me to better accommodation. I felt like Lucy with Mr. Tumnus. I think he the one who, when I doubted if I had strength to make the journey home had said, 'Don't worry! I can carry very heavy wood. I was glad not to take him up on that offer.

There was the night when I was dreaming of rats, kerchiefs on their heads and swords at their belts and woke up to find my meat pie nibbled into. I had been reading too much C.S. Lewis! And always there were headaches and upset tums from the smoke and flies and the exhaustion of slogging through bogs and up mountains.

But there were the occasional lifts in a jeep or on the back of a motor bike. And those pleasant surprises like the time I went to Pastor Parakism's church and his wife welcomed me with clean sheets on my bed and home comforts. She had learned her housekeeping from the missionaries wives at Kandep. And always I could remind the Lord of his promise of 'Peace and joy.' When I was feeling at my lowest the sun would come out, the children responding to God's word and I felt I wouldn't be anywhere else in the world.

They were building roads too throughout the territory, and I would be able to have my own transport. The work could only get easier.

School was over now for the long Christmas holiday. The camp for the young people was great fun and then Mary and I flew to Kopiago to keep Valerie company for a few weeks as the Jourdains were on furlough. Wonderfully, they agreed for Kapusa to join us so I was able to continue my language study and the task of writing Sunday School lessons.

Back to Kurap where Hannah and Masikili were doing well. I could not return as a primary teacher now we had our indigenous teachers trained. Now from there began the long journey home.

From the isolation of Kurap, Laiagam seemed to be a thriving community with several European families and of course the airstrip. On from there to Mount Hagen. This was civilisation. It was strange to see men still wearing tankard leaves queuing up for ice cream. It had been a one horse town when we arrived but was fast growing and there was need of a pastor now to care for all the Apostolics who had come here to work.

On by plane again to Port Moresby. I had thought that I had not wanted to leave New Guinea but when they told me that my vaccination certificate was missing and that I could not fly with out it I realised that there was no returning. This chapter was closed.

'When did you have it?' the doctor asked. A UFM missionary had met us and taken us home for lunch. Now she rushed us across the city to a Christian doctor. The scar had healed but I was able to tell him the date for Val had given it on my birthday. He gave me the precious paper.

I had been amazed at the streets and traffic in Moresby but as we flew low between the sky scrapers of Hong Kong I was awed. I remember trying to describe the London underground to some villagers and they had thought it just a tall, or should I say, deep story. Now I could hardly believe though I was seeing it for myself.

We had a day seeing the sights of Hong Kong. I remember I was delighted by the little button chrysanthemums on the hotel tables, and then, when we reached Athens, to see a little cock sparrow.

Home Again

'Sprechen sie Deutch?' Mary and I had two lovely days with Tel, a Greek friend, and his family and were having our hair set. The lady was determined to make conversation with us somehow and I managed to satisfy her curiosity with my little German.

After thirteen hours on the plane it was a struggle to get our legs to cooperate as we climbed the steps of the Parthenon.

We seemed to be circling London for at least an hour before at last we landed. It was John we saw first. To see a face so familiar, so dear, after the long years was my undoing. The flood gates opened. I remember Mother holding me tight. 'Don't cry, don't cry,' she said, as she used to when as a little child I had fallen and hurt myself.

The whole world seemed a celebration. The daffodils, almond and cherry trees were all in blossom together.

We were not conscious of changing seasons in New Guinea, only of the occasional dry spells when we could run short of water, a and might have frost. Never have I been so thrilled by the miracle of spring as I was that year, to wonder at the unfurling of a million tiny leaves on a beech hedge, and hear the jubilation of a dawn chorus.

I was asked to visit some of the churches to tell of my experiences, and was the guest speaker at the South Wales women's rally, a great honour. After our lives of isolation it wasn't easy to turn public speaker, but a dream had helped me. All these women were crowding around me, so angry, because they couldn't hear what I was saying.

Through this I realised the importance of being strong in the Lord and speaking out a positive message.

When one day Mrs. Bush, hard of hearing said, 'There is one thing. We can always hear our Pauline,' I was so thankful that God had given me that dream.

But I couldn't survive long without earning my way. Any gifts I received must be for New Guinea. Mary and I both returned to teaching, believing that it was only for a short time.

People used to ask me if I saw a lot of difference since I had gone away. Five years is a long time, but I was so happy to find that so much that was dear to me was the same. I had a shock when I found some friends looking so much older, and I'm sure their reaction was the same, but I found it was the same them underneath and they were not really changed. There were new road systems of course. We had to drive an extra mile to reach our home because we could no longer cut across the North Circular, and then the standard of living had definitely risen. Even my mother had central heating and wall to wall carpets, but it is only on looking back that I realise how standards of morality had eroded. Whereas before I left, a pregnancy out of wedlock was reason to lose ones job, now I found myself in schools where most of the staff were living with their boy friends. And whereas the children I had taught in Hoxton had been ignorant of any Christian teaching, many of those I was teaching now had been taught not to believe, and would tell me that Jesus was not true. Multifaith religious teaching was coming in now too.

But we did not think that we would be staying. Mary was busy filling in forms and had been interviewed ready to return to the territory as a secondary school teacher. Then she heard that she was not accepted because she was not divorced, only separated from her husband.

We were both devastated. I was ill in bed with gastric 'flu and the doctor had to give me an injection to bring relief from vomiting. Yes, I was physically ill, but it was a spiritual conflict. I had so believed that this was my life calling and that nothing could prevent my return to the highlands, but deep in my heart came a voice reminding me, Hadn't the Lord asked you to be willing to go anywhere for him? Doesn't anywhere include staying just where you are?

I understood a little of how Abraham felt when God asked him to offer Isaac.

I went to church, not even wanting God to speak. How could I ever trust in prophecy again? But when Pastor Spurdle came up to me after the service and asked me if I would be willing to take up my responsibilities again as a deaconess I was able to tell him, 'Pastor, there is nothing I would like more.'

Yes, I was willing to stay at home, but what about attending the Summer Institute of Linguistics? After all, I was still willing to go anywhere for the Lord.

'That's right, keep moving,' Pastor David Ware told me when I visited them in Dublin. 'When you are moving it is easy for the Lord to give you a push and get you into the right place.'

SIL, run by the Wycliffe Bible Translators, was a wonderful experience. Why hadn't I attended this course before ever setting out for the mission field? They told me so many things that I had had to learn the hard way, but probably I got more out of the course because of my experience abroad. It was there that I met two Apostolic girls, Alice, from Denmark, who went on to marry and has worked for many years in Bible translation in Kenya, and Connie, from Holland, who, working in Ivory Coast often used to visit me in Ghana. ,

'I know a little Pentecostal church that would just suit you.' I didn't have transport so had walked with some others gone to a Methodist church near by but had come home feeling empty and depressed. What a blessing it was to find fellowship in this little AOG church, and I suppose I was a blessing to them.

'You will suffer pain, but I will bring you through.' It was my last service there. The meeting had finished and then there came this word. Surely not for me. But it was.

It was while I was in Kurap that I started to come over sick and faint while out on trek. Then at Kopiago I had been in pain and Val had considered having me flown out to hospital but we called for the elder to pray with us and God answered. I had been ill while itinerating but the doctor had thought it was because of the upheaval in my life. I believe that it was through the blessing of coming to the Lord's Table that I had kept well through the eleven weeks of the Wycliffe course, but now I had to see the doctor.

Jeremy, whom I had known years before in the church in Eastbourne,was now my doctor, and when it was confirmed that I needed an operation he arranged for me to go to the Mildmay mission hospital. What a privilege and blessing. Again I was seeing what God was doing among the people of Hoxton.

'I will lift up my eyes unto the hills....My help cometh from the Lord.' I was just coming round from the anaesthetic when I heard these words. From the ward came the sound of laughter for the nurse on duty had chosen the same passage that morning but I was able to whisper, 'It was specially for me.'

God had spoken to me through this psalm when I first arrived home, telling me that if I would keep looking to him he would make a way for me, step by step. As I waited outside the operating theatre I was able to repeat the whole psalm through and my heart was at peace. But I am glad I did not know of the hard experience that lay ahead.

But let me tell first of how God led me to apply to work with Wycliffe.

One of the hardest things I found about Mary's coming to New Guinea was having to share a bedroom. I had been so used to being on my own and I needed space. You could not even go out for a walk on your own.

Now, at Wycliffe, I was sharing a room with seven others. It was my salvation to walk in the woods for my prayer time. I watched the blackberries develop from hard green knobs to luscious ripe fruit, and sometimes would see a rabbit or fox, but I was walking with the Lord.

I often took a smaller path that later joined up again with the main track. When I felt the Lord calling me to apply to work with Wycliffe I feared that it was like this little path, just a diversion, for after all, I was Apostolic, and my calling was to children's work.

It was a day of prayer. I had missed lunch and again was walking through the woods when I went to higher ground. I found that I was looking down on the path I usually walked and saw that it was not the lesser path that was the diversion. It was the main path that was in a curve. God was showing me that this that he was calling me to was in his will.

'Thank you Lord, It is a straight path.' For over a year I was filling in application forms, writing out doctrinal statements in preparation for going forth again, but meanwhile God had other lessons to teach me.

CHAPTER NINETEEN—IT'S FURTHER ON

I was so glad to wake from this frightening dream. I was alone in the house as my mother had gone to New Zealand to visit Joy. I always locked up carefully, putting the chain on the door, just as she would have done. I had been dreaming that someone was trying to force his way in.

It was only a dream, but I felt depressed and fearful. Then, as I turned on the radio I heard a song, something about, I wanted to come in but your door was locked and barred and you left me outside. It was based on the verse in Revelation of course, 'Behold I stand at the door and knock.'

What is it Lord? I asked, for I realised now that God had been speaking to me through my dream. Then he told me, 'I want to come to you through this experience, but you won't let me.'

The operation! It was true. I had been terrified. Hospitalisation might happen to other people but not me. God would heal me. I felt ill, as much through fear as because of my troublesome gall bladder. But now, as I opened my heart to accept that God was allowing this for good, I had a wonderful experience.

Jeremy, my doctor, had trained at the Mildmay Mission hospital and had been able to arrange for me to go there. If my mother had not been away I could not have accepted, but as it was I was glad to go.

'You are one of us,' one of the local patients told me when she learned that I had been teaching there. Once again I was to see the work the Lord was doing in Hoxton, and even shared a ward with a one time pupil. I made many lovely friends, and eventually was much better in health. But there was convalescence to go through first.

Because there was no one at home I was privileged to go to the Mildmay convalescent home at Worthing. There I met Lily and was told that Ruth, from Australia was over here. It was she who had seen me off at Melbourne station. Eventually we met up. But now it was back to work.

'You must only teach for half a day for the first month.' If only the doctor had known what hardship that meant I'm sure he would not have said it for from then on I was on supply, sent to the worst classes in the worst areas. Some prefer supply teaching, but I need to establish a relationship with the children.

After various hard experiences I was landed with a class of eleven year olds. Near the end of the summer term when they were more than ready to go on to the comprehensive school, with weak nerves after the operation, I felt a total failure.

It was all too much. I was an infant, not a junior teacher. I shouldn't be placed in such a situation. I would go to the office and complain.

I went to the prayer meeting full of self pity, expecting some word of comfort from the Lord. Instead it was rebuke. 'There are some here who are not committed to me.'

I went home and wept. Lord, all I want is to please you and you tell me I am not committed. For yes, I knew he had been speaking to me.

Then God showed me. He was in control. It was he who was allowing these circumstances and I would not accept them.

I didn't go to the office. I returned, confident that, having proved to myself that I was a failure the Lord would now enable me to cope with this difficult class. Instead they were given to a younger teacher while I took some groups. I had to accept this humiliation as God's gift to me, and indeed I believe it was all a part of his equipping me for my work of training others. I was to minister to those who had no confidence in themselves.

But still it continued, moving from school to school. I had just licked one class into shape and organised their work for the morning when I was called to go to another school. It was not yet eleven o'clock. I was exhausted physically and emotionally.

'Lord, I can't face this day.' Driving to yet another school I was reminded of the time there were two mountains to climb to reach home and the Lord had asked me, could I take the next step? By facing a step instead of a mountain I had reached home without being exhausted.

Now he asked me, could I face the next hour? I would not have started teaching by then. Yes, Lord, I can face this next hour. Somehow from then on I was able to cope and even to enjoy teaching again. It seems that God had had to change me before he could change my situation.

My application to Wycliffe was going ahead. Papers were sent for my pastor's approval.

'I can't sign this,' Pastor Hammond told me. 'I will have to take this to council,' for we are a church with central government.

It was our Easter convention. Pastor Leslie Davies, now a beloved brother in law, was one of the speakers. There was a prophetic word, concerning being restored to the place of God's will. I had thought it was for him, for he had gone through an experience of rejection, but it must have been for me too for Pastor Hammond returned from the church council to tell me that they had agreed to send me to Ghana.

I was thrilled, for it was to do the work of Sunday Schools and teacher training that God had shown me while in New Guinea. How wonderfully he was working out his purposed. I would gladly have packed my bags and left straight away. But no, I must wait. The Cawthornes were coming home on furlough and it would not be wise to go without them there to help me to settle in. Eventually I learned it would be a whole year before I could go.

I was frustrated. I don't know why I didn't try to make a start at learning Twi, the language 'of the place where I was going.' For some reason I felt the only thing that could ease my frustration was to take up Greek again. I had been taking a course with London Bible College some years before. I got out all my lesson notes, but where was my Wenham's grammar?

I searched the house, even going into the loft. I had to have it. God had been teaching us to praise him in everything, no matter how wrong they may seem. I praised him now, in my frustration, by faith. Then it came to me. Keith, who had taught with Mary had been to LBC. He would have a copy. I would ask to borrow it. He had left teaching now to work with a missionary society.

'Come over. We would love to see you.'

How I praise God for my missing Wenham, which turned up a few weeks later, inexplicably, in the church vestry, for Keith now gave me invaluable advice.

'You must thank God for this delay,' he told me. 'Contact Scripture Union, Scripture Press, Child Evangelism Fellowship..

anyone who works with children and learn as much as you can from them.'

I attended many courses and gained so much from the wonderful people who led them.

I was accepted for a course with Child Evangelism Fellowship. It meant three months in Switzerland. Since the Lord had delivered me from my fear of mountains I had often longed to go there.

If I could have someone to share the driving I decided I would take the car so that I could visit some of our churches over there. My co-driver however was not a great help. We had been travelling all day. Only then did she announce that she couldn't drive in the dark so I had to do the last weary hours until at last we found the little village of Kilchzimmer.

Because I had transport they had put me to stay in the village. I had thought I had forgotten all my German but by the end of the three months it had come back. Lydia, my room mate, a lovely Swiss WEC missionary, took me to see her parents and was so apologetic that she had left me alone with her mother but we had had no problem with communicating. And when she lost me in the town and asked in a shop if an English lady had come in they told her someone was there who spoke 'written German.' I felt quite chuffed at that.

I found the course intense and very helpful, though I would not go along with all their teaching or methods. But there were other lessons to learn. I was exhausted after the long hours of driving and was expected to take up my duty the next morning, which was stacking and unloading the dishwasher. It was heavy work and I still was not strong.

Then the fellowship was good, but definitely not Pentecostal. We had known blessing and liberty in the Ilford assembly. How could I survive these three months?

The Lord told me, come up into the mountains. Speak in tongues, lift up your hands and praise me as if you were in a great congregation. I was obedient. It wasn't always easy for sometimes my heart was heavy. There was an occasion when I felt I had been falsely accused and misunderstood, but God hadn't changed and so I tried to praise him. But now the rain was coming. I couldn't even have my quiet time. I began to run towards the house but the rain came on so heavily that I had to take shelter under the side of the mountain. Suddenly I found that, like Moses, I was in the cleft of the rock.

I had praised by faith before, but now I felt embraced and overflowing with the glory of God. I went back so full of joy and love that it melted away any misunderstandings. I even found joy in the old dishwasher.

There was another special experience. It was the Sunday of the Penygroes convention, always a special time for our fellowship. I missed breakfast and was walking up into the mountains. These were not the towering heights of the Alps but the gentler mountains of the Bernese Oberland, but there was a spectacular outcrop of rock where people loved to climb to overlook the valleys. It was early and the paths deserted. I made my way to the Belchenflug but as I began to climb I paused. I was afraid.

I had thought that God had delivered me from my fear of heights but had it just been that the mountains of New Guinea were not frightening ones?

Then I saw the steps that were carved into the side. I had a strange feeling I had seen them before. I had, only it had been in a dream, or was it a prophetic picture that the Lord had given me.

I was falling! I awoke with a start to realise I was still in bed, not falling over the cliff at Beachy Head as I had thought. But as I drifted off to sleep it would happen again. We had had a glorious walk over the springy turf, the skylarks thrilling and the tiny scarlet pimpernel and vetch at our feet. I had kept well away from the cliff edge. Nevertheless, such was my fear of heights that now this terrible sensation of falling was tormenting me.

When Pastor Angell returned from a trip to Switzerland, full of the beauties of the Jungfrau, it began again, and I had not even been there myself! But by now I was learning to pray. 'Lord, please deliver me from this fear.'

I saw the steps cut in the side of a mountain. The Lord's arm was around me, and I began to climb. Always there was another step that I could take. I did not dare look down, nor did I need to. I was safe, for God was with me, underneath and around me. We went up through the clouds. Then I looked down to see the world spread out below me and I could not be afraid for I was in Christ in heavenly places. I was never tormented by this fear after that.

Now, remembering my dream, I began to climb, conscious that the Lord was with me, calling me on.

As I stood on that outcrop of rock, like an eagles nest overlooking the land, it was as though all the world was spread before me, and I was in Christ in heavenly places. At first I was clinging on to the rail, but gradually I began to relax as I poured out my praise to the Lord. I hadn't been to the convention but I had my portion of blessing.

I had driven to Bern for a blessed weekend with Pastor Alun Morris, and Veronica and he invited me to the convention but it was the same day as the graduation at Kilchzimmer. Wonderfully, I was given permission to go. I will never forget driving up through the mountains and in the distance I saw rose coloured turrets appearing through the clouds. I thought I was having a glimpse of heaven until I realised that I was seeing the sun lighting up the Alps.

We were nearing the end of the course with CEF. My co-driver had already left. I was sick with worry at the thought of that long journey back on my own, but I had a heavenly Father who was pledged to look after his child. He could either provide a co-driver, or give me grace to do it alone.

A sweet Indonesian girl asked for a lift. At least I would have company, and we had friends who had offered us to stay overnight in Paris.

'Paris? When will you be there?' A young Apostolic from New Zealand had been hitch hiking his way across Europe, and would be in Paris the same night on his way to UK. What a wonderful God we have.

We had deliberately chosen the longest land route because I am not a good sailor and were praising the Lord when we were the last car onto the ferry but alas, a storm blew up and we were delayed six hours before we could land. I know now that the Lord not only delivers from home sickness, but seasickness as well.

Now I was all set to leave for Ghana. Sandals and cotton dresses this time, and food. We were told that because of economic difficulties in Ghana we must take as much as we could.

'O yammy ye, O yammy ye.' Everyone in our church knew that chorus. I had been learning some Asante Twi, for the Lord had said to learn the language 'in the place where you are going,' and suddenly I realised that it was 'Onyame,' the word for God. Yes, it was a Ghanaian song. Onyame ye - God is good.

I had been visiting a Ghanaian couple living in Kennington who had been teaching me, and now at last it was time for me to go.

I left Heathrow with Philip and Netta Cawthorne and their children, Julie and Mark. It was 29th September 1975. This was to be a new chapter in my life.

CHAPTER TWENTY—MOTHER OF MANY CHILDREN

The traffic was grinding and roaring past us, fumes belching in our faces as we tried to push the car up a steep hill. Turning so that I could push with my back side in order to give my arms a rest, I saw a slogan on one of the mammy lorries that passed us. 'HAD I KNOWN!' I couldn't help but laugh.

It had been a hot and weary journey, with difficulties even before we reached Accra. It was in the steaming heat of the airport at Cairo, with nothing to drink and workmen crashing around us that Netta gave me 'The story of a green shield stamp,' a poem that Pastor Luther Phillips had written about how all the church had rallied to buy my car with these trading stamps.

How I laughed. God has wonderful ways of giving refreshment at the weariest moments. We eventually arrived in Accra with its imposing buildings and broad tree lined streets and the women in their bright cloths. We continued on to make the long dusty journey to Kumasi with a car that was objecting to having been neglected for so long. We had to pray it up the hills.

We had arrived at the Cawthornes house in Kumasi in a tropical downpour to find rain pouring in. How thankful we were when David Mills arrived, an 'Elim angel' working with the Church of Pentecost. Having helped us to catch the leaks, he took us back to his family for a meal.

The talk was all of the shortages in the country. My stomach knotted. How would I survive? But the verse came to me, 'Your heavenly Father knows that you have need of these things,' and I was to prove his provision. On one occasion when there was no bread, and certainly no flour to make your own, the words slipped into my heart, 'Your bread and water will be sure,' and yes, someone turned up with a loaf. It is good to have to pray for these things and not take them for granted.

There were times when the water supply was cut off, because of shortage of the necessary chemicals. I had thought that I could use river water for my washing but the doctor warned me that this could lead to river blindness. One night I awoke to hear the rain beating on the roof so I rushed outside to fill some buckets, tripping over a concrete flour pot. I retired to nurse my wounds, cold and wet and still with no water.

On one occasion I shared, 'The electricity and water is on, I have petrol in my tank and bread in my fridge. What more can I want?' I was learning to count my blessings.

The Lord had provided a house for me at the other side of the city and after just a few weeks with the Cawthornes my loads and my 'green shield' Ford Escort arrived and I was able to set up home.

I had realised that my work would now be centred in the cities, but my original call had been to the villages and I was so happy that I was living where there was a village atmosphere. Oduom was a suburb of Kumasi so I had the advantage of electricity and running water, well, some of the time. St. Louise girls' school was a stone's throw away so there were educated and some English people within reach, yet I was living in the atmosphere of a village, where only Twi was spoken.

I had a wonderful welcome from the pastors and members of the Apostolic church in Kumasi. The young people, already enthused by the Child Evangelism Fellowship missionary who had visited there, were rearing to go and soon had me involved in visiting different Sunday Schools, taking teacher training classes, and speaking at rallies. I saw now God's goodness in the delay and that I had attended the course in Switzerland.

Soon after my return from New Guinea there had been prophecy that I would go forth again and be the mother of many children. Now I was welcomed as the children's mother, Adwoa London, mother of thousands.

It was Joseph, my house boy, and his elder brother, who asked if they might call me 'Maame Adwoa.' Born on a Monday, Adwoa was my day name. Soon I was known throughout the church as Maame Adwoa Thompson.

We had a women's convention soon after I arrived. I will never forget the sight of those thousands and thousands of women, in their bright cotton cloths, many with babies on their backs, under that vast awning. It was wonderful to see them dancing in the open space in front of the platform, and then the pastors had to have their turn. This was something I had not expected, but dancing was part of their way of life.

'Come on, Madam, please dance with us.' It was Mary, such a dear sister, who often used to interpret for me.

'Oh Mary, I'm sorry, I can't.' I was far too self conscious. It was reading about Richard Wurmbrant that first convicted me that I should be willing to dance before the Lord. He danced in prison, with chains on his feet, because he believed that we should worship God with every part of our being. When in Switzerland I used to go up into the mountains to have my quiet time. I had felt then that I should not only raise my hands and my voice but dance to the Lord but oh, suppose someone saw me? And then years ago I had had a dream.

Night after night I had been having nightmares. I asked God to give me a happy dream and he did. I was dancing and dancing. I awoke, full of joy, and I always felt that sometime my dream would become reality, but oh - not now, Mary.

Well, if I didn't have courage to dance with the women, at least I could dance before the Lord. I began to dance in my bedroom when I was having my prayer time. I felt stupid and self conscious but it was a matter of obedience. Then one day I forgot myself and danced and danced, full of joy, worshipping the Lord.

'I want you to dance before my people.'

'Oh no Lord.' I wept. I couldn't. Then I realised, God wouldn't ask me to do anything that would embarrass people. If he wanted me to do it he would make it a blessing. Years before, he had asked me to sing. I never feel I have a solo voice, but he always makes it a blessing.

Then one Saturday I was at a local women's rally, under the shade of some trees. I would never have a better opportunity.

'They are going to dance. Please dance with us,' Mary begged.

'Oh, I'm sorry.' I watched as the women tripped off the platform until I realised that I would be left up there alone with the pastor. I pulled out my handkerchief and tripped after them. I've never been light on my feet but now they became like feathers. I was worshipping the Lord in the dance, and my sisters were so delighted.

I shall never forget the look of surprise and joy on the face of Isobel, an Anglican missionary that I had invited to one of our leadership training courses. She came in as we were all dancing and singing, filled with the joy of the Lord. But that comes in the next chapter.

I drove into town, teaching at our Bible college twice a week, teaching English as well as on children's work. I had always felt safe teaching the little ones and had wondered how I would cope with adults, but now I found I had the same happy relationship that I had had with my infants. One day I referred to the Sunday School scholars as being my children and one pastor, probably as old as I was, said, 'Oh Maame Adwoa, they must be your grandchildren, because you are our mother.' How rich I was.

I would go on from there to do my shopping. There was scarcely anything to buy in Kingsway, but outside the boys were selling fruit and vegetables. I used to dread going there for they were all mobbing me, pressing me for their custom.

'Lord, you want me to serve you joyfully. Please help me to do my shopping joyfully too.' The situation changed completely. John informed me that he was a Christian and would look after me. I found the stall where Papa Duku sold cloth and would call in for some fellowship. I was actually enjoying my trips to town!!

The Africans do not like to think of anyone being alone and Papa Duku offered for his youngest daughter, Deborah to come and live with me, and so for a little while I was a 'joyful mother of children,' especially when Elizabeth, Pastor Antwi's daughter came too and with Joseph there as well. However, with the tremendous pressures of coping with a tropical climate, a country in economic difficulties and the many demands of my work, it was a lot having to drive Deborah to and fro to school, and I really needed to be able to escape to my splendid isolation. It wasn't easy for either of us, and dear Papa Duku was wise enough to understand.

It was while Deborah was with me that the church folk at last found me a watchman. They had insisted that I should have one and no, it was not a work that Christians did. It was scary to have a foreigner (he came from the north of Ghana) passing close beneath our window, and when we drove home from a watch night service to find someone lying fast asleep on the apron of my garage, his club at the ready, we were scared to wake him in case he thought we were the intruders.

After that I insisted that I would rather be without a watchman. I did not have much of this worlds goods so was not likely to be targeted by the armed robbers who were on the prowl.

'Oh, Miss Thompson, what is it?' I never did discover what kind of night creature it was that made the terrible wailing. We used to say that it sounded like a baby being murdered, something that came back to haunt me when there was a tragedy just a stones throw away. Deborah crept into bed beside me. Living in a busy suburb of Kumasi, she was not used to the noises of the countryside.

Which did you prefer, New Guinea or Ghana? People have often asked me that. I can only say that when I was there I would not have been anywhere else in the world. We did not have the spectacular scenery or mountains of New Guinea, but nor did we have the mud and fleas and rats. The Ghanaians are so clean in their persons, and wonderful cooks.

I had my 'Good news' car, as they called it. 'Good News!' with the response 'Christ died for my sins' was the Sunday School slogan. But I found that I would be just as exhausted by travelling in the heat as I had been by climbing a mountain in New Guinea. But here again in Ghana I was at home and had a wonderful sense of fulfilment.

If only I could have a quiet day at home to get on with my preparation, I used to think when I had to drive into town for this and that. Suddenly I had all the time in the world, for my car that had been so special, was a write off.

It was only a few weeks before that a young Ghanaian, William had died. A faithful Apostolic, he worked at the university, just three miles away, and had a motor bike. I used to call him 'My Brother John,' because he always came when something was needed, like John at home. One Whit Sunday he and another young man had danced before the Lord. I've never seen anyone dance as William did. When I heard of his sudden and inexplicable death I knew that he was dancing in heaven.

Driving home after a happy weekend in Accra I had suddenly seen this large Mercedes careering toward me. I was probably unconscious for some moments, but as I came to I felt that the gates of heaven had been shut in my face.

'Lord' I said, 'you took William but you didn't take me.' The answer was clear, 'Because of the children.'

I struggled to get out of the car and sat on the verge. I felt so alone. 'Lord, you must send someone to help me.'

Just then two high ranking army officers drove up, and took control of the situation. They took us all to hospital, contacting Pastor Williams, helping him to get the car towed to a police station and eventually negotiating so that the case was settled out of court, a wonderful blessing for me.

As I lay in hospital, the people peeping round the screens in curiosity at seeing a white woman, I remembered the little child who had been dancing in church the day before. Children often want to show off and their parents will stop them but this toddler had been worshipping the Lord. As I lay there I knew that God was good.

It was a private hospital, the doctor had a German wife, and I was sent a beautiful meal, though I couldn't eat much. But lack of toilet facilities was one reason why they packed me off to be cared for by Sylvia. A fortnight of tender loving care and they brought me back to Oduom.

I was shocked, had a bashed face, and a badly bruised arm, which eventually pushed me into learning to touch type instead of using two fingers on the typewriter, but now I was glad to be back in the village. Instead of rushing here and there I had time to visit the people, learning their culture as well as their language. Philip used to bring Julie to the school next door so would bring me my mail, and I could have a lift with him into the Bible School when I was teaching. I could always get a taxi back from town.

I did savour the delights of public transport for, so far from town, it was nothing to wait half an hour for a taxi. On one occasion I accepted a lift in a mammy lorry. Never again. In a long skirt, which I often wore, I could climb up, but how to get down again was another thing. Then there was the tro-tro, or mini-bus. You thought it was full when you got in but every time another passenger hailed them we all had to shove up. Ever thought you were a sardine?

'She's a teacher at St. Louise,' one told the other in Twi when I accepted a lift in a taxi. When I corrected him, in English, there was stunned silence. Then they began to discuss, could I have understood them? But sometimes when I got into a tro-tro the word would go round, this is the white woman who speaks our language. I still felt a beginner, but that was encouraging.

It was difficult to get a language teacher to come as far out as Oduom, but there was a class at the Tech, (University of Science and Technology). Two SIM missionaries joined us.

'We can see that you are serious, like us. Would you like to come to our house for extra lessons?' Would I? They became wonderful friends, and when I had no transport would sometimes bring the teacher out to me.

The children from the village used to love to come and visit me. On one occasion I told Joseph to send them away as I was busy but he told me that they would not believe that I had said such a thing. I asked them in and they sang to me and I prayed with them and they were satisfied. Like the disciples, I learned that I must never send the children away.

This was the beginning of our Sunday School which became such a blessing, for now when I taught the teachers I was able to talk, not about experiences in UK or New Guinea, but of what I had learned in teaching Ghanaian children.

I had learned to visualise songs and texts while in Switzerland, but now I had to do everything in Twi. I can remember searching my heart to know what 'Christ in you' really meant to me before I could teach it to the childen. I realised that it meant that when I was driving alone in the car, meeting with officialdom where the white man was no longer always respected, or in other frightening situations, that Jesus was that friend alongside. It is good sometimes to have to translate what you believe.

My house was on the main Accra to Kumasi road. Sometimes I had warning, but it was always a joy when visitors turned up. If I wasn't in, Joseph would make them welcome. Two single 'girls', WEC missionaries from the north, where life was much harder, came at different times to spend their week's holiday with me. There was a conference at WEC on cassette ministry. I had visitors staying with me for this when I was shocked to hear that Mary had to have a very big operation for a brain tumour. It was wonderful that I was not on my own and that a telegram arrived the same day to say that she was safely through it. Only God could have arranged that. However, I was still very anxious.

'It is at times like this that you are always filled with regrets,' a friend shared.

'It is at times like this that you really prove whether you believe that God forgives sins,' I told her. I had prayed so much that as God was healing Mary's marriage, that he would heal her physically, for she had been becoming more and more disabled. I should have had faith but now I was so afraid that she would die. One night, alone again, the dam burst. My neighbours heard me crying and came in to comfort me and the next day Joseph went to fetch the Cawthornes and they took me to see a doctor.

I was on medication for a few days but then I was prayed for and felt I did not need it. Ernest had asked if I might have an early furlough but the response was negative and then the news came that my new car was on the way. I had thought I would never have courage to drive again after the accident, but now I was fine. Once again I was fully involved, travelling to different rallies and conventions as well as working in the district.

I had gone to the conference on cassette ministry, not sure that it had anything to do with me, but God showed me that this was a way that I could reach my teachers and a small band of us had great joy in working on this, and Florence Yeboah was such an inspiration to us as she helped us to make the recording.

The tropical climate was debilitating and we all used to go down with bugs and wogs, but now I seemed to be feeling increasingly unwell. I used to long to be slim but I was losing so much weight that I was afraid I would go down the plug hole. For once I had plenty of food in my fridge, for my Wycliffe friends had driven through from the Ivory Coast and brought us a good supply, but alas, now I had lost my appetite. As for having a tan, my skin looked plain dirty to me. Of course, I was turning yellow and ended up in hospital with hepatitis.

The Cawthornes were packing up ready to go on furlough, and now on top of this had to bring meals for me into the hospital, but the doctor's wife was English and helped out, not that I had much appetite.

I was so grateful for those who came to visit me, though when I asked the pastors to pray that I wouldn't have to have any more injections, Pastor Mante informed me that I wasn't in heaven yet.

Mary Nsiah was one of my most capable Sunday School teachers, and if I had had a 'Brother John,' now I had a 'Sister Mary.' She would come in, tidy my locker, make my bed and do those little things that only a sister can do. How I praise God for being in such a wonderful family.

I had to laugh though when I asked Joseph to bring me some books from the library. He brought me Dickens, as I had requested, but alas, it was an easy read version that was suitable for him, not me. I was so disappointed.

At last it was agreed that I should return to UK. This was the only time I had to fly alone, after my initial journey to New Guinea, but I was feeling so poorly that I did not worry about company.

On the plane, we were approaching Heathrow when I looked out of the window to see the shadow of our plane thrown onto a cloud. It was within the circle of a rainbow.

I had been feeling such a failure, not even able to complete a two year term. Had I accomplished anything? But now God was telling me that I was in his hand, in the centre of his will and all was well.

The 'Good News' car, with children from my village by the University

CHAPTER TWENTY ONE—STILL FURTHER ON?

'Maame Adwoa-eh!' Yes, I was home in Oduom at last. More than a year since I left, they must have wondered whether I would be back, as indeed I had done.

My illness had been so debilitating, though they had assured me that I had not had it seriously. A young man had died of hepatitis while I was in the hospital. I had been preparing to return to Ghana but Grace, a nurse friend, realising I was not fit, begged me to ask for another check up. The doctor then insisted I had another six months.

I was very upset at the time, though looking back we realised that other things would not have fallen into place if I had gone back earlier.

I kept busy while I was at home, involved in the church life as always, but had to make sure I did not get overtired. I visited my many friends that I had made when teaching and, wondering if I would ever get back to Ghana, thought of returning to teaching. Then at least I would be doing something with my life.

That night Pastor Douglas preached on Elisha burning his plough when Elijah called him to full time ministry, and I knew that it was a word for me. There was to be no return to secular work.

At last the date was fixed. Pastor and Mrs Chivers would be travelling out with me. I had wondered how I could face the loneliness again so was grateful for their company, but after a few weeks of having them share my small house and all the pressures of life in general I realised that God was giving me his best in letting me live on my own.

Joseph was a young man now and had found other work so Yaw Boakyi, one of the many children next door, began to come in and help me. I used to try to speak Twi with Joseph but it had been easy to slide into English. Now it was Twi all the time. I felt ashamed when I helped Yaw to get into a better school. The teachers had thought that working for a 'Bruni,' (a white woman) that his English would have been good.

'Come on, we will have an English lesson.' I decided I must do more to help him, but Yaw had other ideas. 'Oh, but I am going to teach you to break proverbs.' If you could use their many proverbs you really knew their language.

I had not known what to do about starting the local Sunday School again without Joseph's help, but it was taken out of my hand. One Sunday afternoon I was wondering whether I had courage to drive into Kumasi for the evening service when I saw a flock of children coming from the village, all bathed and in their best clothes. 'Maame Adwoa, we have come for Sunday School.' I managed without an interpreter, and went on from there. It is around some of the wonderful things that God did in the lives of these children that I have written Gift of Gold.

But what of my work of training the Sunday School teachers? I had attended other training courses while I was home and been up to visit them at Scripture Union. I became convinced that the way for the work to prosper was through leadership training courses. There were so many obstacles to overcome but wonderfully it worked out.

One day, after teaching at the college, I went up to share my concern with Pastor Ofori Addo. I felt a fool when I began to weep, but the burden was so heavy. It was Missionary Prayer Meeting Monday. The work seemed to open up from there.

The highlight for me was the training weekend in Kumasi. The young people took hold of the teaching from the word of God and were filled with faith. They learned that we can bring our needs to the Lord and claim the promises in his word. The next time we met they were all praising God for answered prayers.

One young pastor said, 'I used to be interested in children's work, but now I have a vision.'

It was there that Isobel had come in when we were all dancing in worship, the Lord filling us with joy.

I used to teach them to make simple visual aids. Some of them had bought flannelgraphs from CEF but I had not met one who had even cut them out and so many could not afford them. We would find a special stone to tell the story of the treasure in the field, a branch to make a tree for Nicodemus to sit under and it was easy to get a lamp or some bread and fish in a little basket. They too were full of ideas. One teacher made a wonderful well in a bucket for the woman of

Samaria, and when they acted the parable of the debtors we had all the trappings of the Asante Hene, King of Ashante.

We would have lectures through Friday evening and Saturday, with plenty of activity and visual aids. Then on Sunday morning we brought the children in and the teachers would each have a group.

'O Maame Adwoa, I thought that you could not teach little children, but they can understand.'

Many years ago there had been a word that we would know 'days of heaven on earth.' Looking back I believe that I experienced that as the leaders' hearts were set alight to teach the children. We were all so filled with joy.

'Madam, where are you going?' I was setting out for a teachers' meeting, but when Yaw Boakyi realised that I was going into town at night on my own he called me into the house. 'We must pray.'

I shall never forget the fervour of this young boy. He was concerned for me that I should be kept safe, but he was telling the Lord of the importance of my work and bringing to God the verses which I used with the teachers. He had accompanied me on some occasion and they were hidden in his heart.

I was never well, often feeling as if I were running a temperature when I set out on these special weekends. I didn't know whether it was nerves, or whether the enemy was attacking. But now I had been away for one of these special weekends and had returned with a tummy bug. Having had hepatitis I hadn't built up any reserves and felt that I was back again to square one. But before I had left UK I had had a very special word that I had hidden in my heart.

I was a speaker in the missionary meeting at the Kennington convention just prior to my return. It was there that God gave me a word through Pastor Granville Johnson, based on the verse in 3 John. He told me, 'You are in my hand, and it was in my hand that you should prosper and be in health as your soul prospers.' I hadn't shared my concern about my health, but God had known and come to reassure me. Now I used to visit the assemblies and tell them of this promise to me. 'But if you haven't a good Sunday School then I am not prospering,' I would tell them, 'because I am the Sunday School mother.'

But now I felt so weak and ill. What of the Lord's promise?

My SIM friends took me to the doctor and kept me with them. A missionary from Nigeria was passing through and stayed a night.

He asked if he might massage my feet. I know some people have reservations about reflexology, but all I know is that after he had ministered to me I fell into a deep refreshing sleep and awoke much better and went on from there, although I still often felt that I had no reserve of strength.

But suddenly my plans were brought to a full stop. Once again there was a petrol shortage. My Father in heaven was pledged to meet my need. He could guide me so that I would not have to queue for a long time. I went on into town after teaching in the Bible School, full of faith that God would direct me to a petrol station where a supply had just come in, but after queueing all afternoon in the terrific heat as well as the hassle - queuing is something different in Africa - I drove home, putting the car in the garage. What was I to do? I did not dare go out to queue again for if I ran out of petrol I could not leave the car unattended.

There were terrible things going on in Ghana at that time. There had been coups before, but the corruption had continued. Now they were determined to stamp it out. At first the people rejoiced, until we began to realise that there were none of us who were not guilty. There were public floggings and houses pulled down. I saw someone with his fingers bandaged and dared not ask what had happened. My heavenly Father had seen that it was best for me to be safely shut up in my village at such a time. Can you imagine my feelings when I went to visit a friend at the University to be told that she had returned to England with her children. 'I'm not having my family molested,' her husband told me. What about me, I thought, when distilling through my mind came a word from many years ago, 'No man will touch you.'

A friend had thought the word of prophecy had been concerning me, and that it meant that I would not marry, but now, all these years later, I realised its significance. I knew that I could claim this promise. I would not be molested. No one would touch me to harm me.

I had been so moved when Mrs Ofori Addo, unable to get a taxi, walked all those miles from town to visit me, a loaf of bread smuggled under her cloth. She was risking a flogging, as she had paid more than the fixed price.

Still Further On?

I had so many wonderful friends that I fear to mention names lest I leave any one out, but I have to mention Victoria. It was she who had taken it on herself to accompany me on my journeys.

It had been a problem for me. The Ghanaians were not happy for me to travel alone, but my superintendent did not approve of me giving lifts. But what was I to do? It was so difficult to get transport, and besides that, to refuse a request was not acceptable in their culture.

There was one occasion when a pastor had asked for a lift to Accra. I didn't know what or who to try to please. 'Lord,' I prayed, 'if this is best, then see that he won't turn up to meet me.' With no telephone, it would be easy enough for this to happen, but there he was, all happy and bright.

'O Maame Adwoa, we must just stop to greet this brother.' Ghanaian customs are delightful, if you are used to the heat, and time is of no consequence as with them. We got a wonderful welcome, and had gifts pressed upon us as is another of their winsome ways, but I realised then that it was better for me to be free when I could.

But now it was wonderful to have Victoria's company on my many journeys, and she not only saw to my food and such but, a capable women's leader, she helped me in the lectures and would give a demonstration lesson for me. When the car was in need of repair, as it very often was with the bad roads, I would stay with her in the church house next to the Bible college until it came back. Though food was so difficult to come by she always had a tasty meal for me, and indeed for everyone who came to her house.

Some retired SIM missionaries were over here visiting their family at the time of the coup. They had a special wedding anniversary and they fetched me for their meal at the City Hotel. I have never forgotten the taste of butter and a freshly baked roll that we had to go with the soup. What a wonderful evening in the midst of all the darkness. It was they who, having queued long hours for petrol came and filled my tank and got the car going again. I felt they were giving of their life blood.

Connie, and her partner Liz, had invited me to join them in Ivory Coast for Christmas. There were the inevitable difficulties of travelling and I arrived minus my suitcase, but it was wonderful to enjoy the prosperity of Abijan, a beautiful modern city, built beside a lagoon. We had a few days at the Wycliffe centre, where I met David

Bendor Samuel and we discussed the possibility of my working for a degree, and then we travelled up into the mountains where was a holiday village built for a retreat for missionaries.

Rising early I would walk outside for my quiet time. The mountains reminded me so much of New Guinea. I had never put it out of my head that I might one day return and now as I felt the Lord speaking to me about preparing to hand over my work to the Africans I presumed that it would be to go back there.

Life was easier when I returned to Kumasi but now I had to start preparing for furlough. It had been simpler in New Guinea for I had gone thinking that it might be for life. I had not dared to even think about returning to UK but now with doing two years at a time, necessary because of the unhealthy climate, we didn't seem to belong anywhere. When we came to UK people said, 'You must be longing to go back,' and the Ghanaians knew that the difficulties we shared were not permanent for us.

Now I was planning for Easter. The national convention was a great event when, in spite of the difficulties of transport, thousands would gather and it was my opportunity to meet with many of the Sunday School teachers. Of course I must return for at least one more term, but I wanted to start to hand over responsibility to the Ghanaians. At present I was a figure head. They wanted me to lead all the meetings, but I felt that I should be as a conductor, coordinating the efforts of these zealous and capable young people.

In some respects life was returning to normal after the coup. The army road block on my way into town had been removed. My heart had always raced when I was called to halt, though my greeting in Twi usually brought a friendly response.

We were issued with petrol coupons, and sometimes an allowance of sugar or other commodities, but still there were shortages and long queues. I tried to take a photo of an extra long queue surreptitiously, from the car. I thought it would help people at home to pray, but the next thing I knew I was taken to see the sergeant. Fortunately we were able to get hold of the local pastor who spoke up on my behalf and I was released on condition that I destroyed the slide.

We had a ladies' Bible study once a fortnight, which was a life line to me. We had no Apostolic missionaries in Kumasi now and though I loved the Ghanaians it was a blessing to meet with those of my own culture. God showed us that we were to share our needs and to pray specifically for each other. I had only to share a concern with them and the Lord would answer.

One day Amy was taking us through Exodus, speaking of Jesus as the water of life. She asked us each to write on a paper something that we were thirsty for. Then we were to take a paper at random and pray for each other's need. I remember the one I took was, 'I am so thirsty for a meaningful quiet time.' But from somewhere deep inside me came the cry, 'I'm so thirsty for love.' Well, I thought, I'm certainly not going to write than down. 'If you don't cry, I can't answer.' How glad I am now that I was obedient.

A week or two before I had heard that my younger sister Joy was engaged. I had been praying for her. She had never been able to accept being single as I had and I prayed the Lord would give her joy. This I believed to be God's answer. I suppose it was this news that had stirred my emotions.

Some American girls recently arrived were sharing accommodation with single men. I went to their leader to express my concern. 'I'm happy to be single,' I told her, 'but it doesn't get any easier.' I felt a fool that my eyes had filled up with tears.

There had been something else which, though I had thought I had dismissed it, had probably stirred me up too. I had had a light hearted proposal of marriage, light hearted because he had known what the answer would be.

Some of the married men in our fellowship used to tease me, making out that I was a peach or a plum or such, and I accepted it as their way of trying to let me know that I was not single because I was unattractive. When a fatherly figure told me that he loved me I replied that I thrived on a bit of love. I had no idea of the unhappiness of his own marriage or of the fire that was burning in his heart, but eventually he made it known.

It was at the time that my father was dying, and I suppose I was especially vulnerable. It is wonderful to know that you are loved, and great pain to be unable to satisfy the one who loves. I am so thankful that God has given us plain 'road signs,' and that we knew that this was a 'no through road,' thankful too that God saved me from wrecking my life. I believe it was he who gave me the wisdom to tell this one, 'There is only one way that you can prove you love me, and that is by never declaring it.' He did prove his love.

Now he was a widower, but in no way could he fit into my life as a missionary. I thought no more about it, yet where had this cry come from?

I did meet a prosperous looking gentleman in the village one day who, delighted that I greeted him in Twi, informed me that he would like to marry me.

'Oh,' I replied, 'unless you ask my father.' For such occasions, Papa Duku, Deborah's father, was my covering. But of course there was no emotional involvement on that occasion. I had taken it as bit of fun, but now this cry has arisen from the depths.

I was so glad that it was Amy who had taken my paper. A sweet young mother, I had met her the day her third child was born and we had had language studies together.

'Now don't go praying that I'll get married,' I told her. 'I'm content as I am.' Apart from my ministry to the children, and to the pastors and beautiful young people who were all my family, I felt I had often been able to help other single women. But then I went to the Ho convention and preached on marriage!!! 'I have a problem in relationship,' I shared with Isobel. Having a hard time, she often called to visit me. 'I'm sure it must be all my fault,' I went on.

'That's funny,' she replied. 'When I have a problem I'm always sure that it's the other persons fault.'

Of course she wasn't right, and neither was I. But when you are far from home and in poor health these matters can seem like mountains. I was condemning myself that I didn't have the courage to sort them out until one day I had a letter with an underlying message that the writer understood my situation and did not condemn me. God spoke through that and I went round the house singing, 'There is no condemnation.'

I turned to this passage in Romans 8 and there the message unfolded, of the unhappy marriage of those under the law and the wonderful relationship that we have in Christ where he encourages us to do better, but never never condemns us.

I went to the Ho convention, not having prepared to speak in Twi, as it was another language area, but Twi was understood throughout Ghana, and 'Oh, Maame Adwoa, you must speak in Twi.'

I arrived from the rest house on the Sunday morning having forgotten my Bible and notes, but I borrowed a Twi Bible and the Lord helped me wonderfully.

'I know what you are thinking. As for you, Maame Adwoa, you are not even married. How can you speak about marriage?' I began and went on to expound these wonderful chapters.

But it was even more amusing when, having left Ghana with every intention of returning, I went to a women's rally in Kennington and told them that I was going to speak about marriage, for by now I had a ring on my finger.

Philip Cawthorne and myself at the Bible School, Kumasi

CHAPTER TWENTY TWO— HOME AGAIN

My tale is nearly told, for I have returned from my wanderings. I marvel that someone so ordinary as I have had such a privilege to take the wings of the morning and in the far off places prove that even there God's hand has been holding me. 'I'm sure you're looking forward to going back.' It was Jackie, a fellow missionary, who was asking.

I had always had joy in my missionary work, but no. I had to confess that I was not. I could not understand it.

Then it came to my interview with the committee. I told them that I was finding it hard, but that I had no other calling. Yes, I was prepared to return.

I had asked them for a new car. How could I face all the hardship caused by a car constantly breaking down? I was learning to always park on a slope because I needed a new battery. Since it had been in 'dry dock' during the coup everything seemed to be going wrong with it. And I wanted to employ a driver. I shall never forget the eight or was it ten hours of driving to Winneba, when I still was not fully recovered, only to be expected to drive around the town to greet the different ones. Oh, for bed, but no. I had visitors, and then, because they had run out of petrol, was expected to drive them home. Shattered, I took a sleeping tablet, something I had not done since my time in hospital, but was rudely awakened from my drugged sleep in the middle of the night with rain pouring on my bed. Never again. In spite of all it was a wonderful weekend.

Strangely I was not too discouraged by the committee's refusal. I knew the Lord could provide, as indeed he did, but in a way that was far from my expectations.

It was soon after I arrived home that we heard the sad news of the sudden death of Joel's wife, and that he was returning home. Mary and I both used to write to Betty when they were in Nigeria, through the pen and prayer league. Since then we had exchanged twice yearly prayer letters. Now Mary and I each wrote to Joel letters of condolence.

Home Again

Busy travelling the country and speaking in the various churches, I was in Bradford when Mary sent on a joint reply from him as he didn't have my address. At the end was a P.S. 'Pauline, you will be interested to know that I have just got my Bachelor of Theology.' I was thrilled, especially as I was hoping to study for a degree, and I remembered that ten years earlier when we were at Bradford together, Joel had been buying books to prepare for his GCE.

I heard that he too would be in Bradford for an interview, but I did not expect to see him. It was my fiftieth birthday, twenty five years since I was received as a member in the Apostolic Church.

I did see Joel. We were all invited out to lunch with the committee, and I just had a chance to congratulate him on his 'p.s.' 'We'll keep in touch,' he said as he left.

I was due to go to Wales, while Joel was going on to visit his in-laws in Scotland. Pastor and Mrs Spurdle had asked me to stay with them, to save me changing beds every night, and drove me to the various meetings each night. They talked a lot about Joel and his dear Mam. They were so concerned for them. They also fed me on honey. Pastor was sure that had something to do with it.

One morning I shared with Sonia my dream; a room full of Apostolics. Betty was there and out of all those people she came up and threw her arms around me.

'Wouldn't you like to be married?' Sonia asked. She could see what was happening.

'I would love to be married,' I told her, 'but my missionary call has to come first.' Even as I said it I realised, no, it is not my missionary call, it is the Lord. 'Your calling is not to a person or to a place, it is a joyful abandonment to your God.' That was the word God had given me so long ago.

I went to speak in Bridgend. Joel was home after all, for it had not been convenient for him to go to Scotland, and was there with his mother and his sister in law, Eunice,also tragically bereaved. His younger brother David had died suddenly, just six months before Betty. Joel spoke to me briefly. The next night we met in Cornelly, his home assembly and I was sitting next to his Mam. I shared with him now my own purpose to study for a degree.

'You could do it with the University of South Africa,' he told me, but I was on my way from there to Birmingham to visit my friend

Joan, and for an interview with the Birmingham Bible Institute. I had thought I would be studying with them but found it was not a degree course. 'You can do it through London Bible College.'

As soon as I was back home I phoned LBC, for I must soon be packing, and needed to take the necessary books with me.

I was the whole morning on the phone, for LBC did not yet have this course available for correspondence. Frustrated, I went and knelt by my bed. 'Lord, is it you who want me to do this or is it just my own idea?' I opened my Bible and read, 'Seek wisdom, seek knowledge.' 'But Lord, every door I have tried is closed.' Then it came to me, the University of South Africa.

Joel meanwhile was praying for a partner. It had been Betty's wish that if anything happened to her that he should marry again and he felt he could not pastor a church on his own. He had thought it impossible that I would give up my missionary call for him, but when I phoned he began to think the impossible possible and this was the beginning of the end, or rather - of a new beginning.

He wrote me a long letter all about my studies, but at the end he wrote,'P.S. It would have been a great delight if our paths should have run parallel.' He was putting into words the prophetic picture the Lord had given me so many years ago, and Pastor Spurdle spoke along these lines at our wedding.

'Could you wait until next week for me to get your drums?' Pastor Douglas had asked. We found reconditioned oil drums ideal for packing our goods, and it was time for me to start. But by the time next week had come I no longer needed them.

It wasn't easy for me to give up my missionary call. It was the doctor at Mildmay who helped me to see that we do not always feel that our work is finished, and counselled me to open my heart to this new experience.

Joel was nine years older than I. Was this just to be for a time and then I would return abroad? God spoke to us, in the prayer meeting at Cornelly, setting my heart at rest, that our work abroad was finished and that God would use us in a great way in this land. I knew now that this was a life commitment, for the picture the Lord had given me was of us walking together into the glory.

We were married in Ilford, my home church. It was Pastor Joshua McCabe, my Australian Dad, over on a visit, who gave me away. The Wallaces were there from Zimbabwe and Ruth from

Australia, now married to Pastor Corr, as well as many other dear friends.

'You have shown me the path of life. You will make me full of joy by your countenance.'

That was the verse on my calendar that morning. After fifty years walking alone I didn't find marriage easy, but it is the most worthwhile thing I have ever done, and I am still full of joy.

I always say that I didn't fall in love until after we were engaged, for I didn't have time before. I was due to return to Ghana in a few weeks so we had to make up our minds right away.

'I'm afraid you love me too much,' Joel told me one day, but I replied, 'I can never love you too much, for in loving you I am loving the Lord.' Yes, I was sure that it was God's will to marry Joel, and that in this too I was choosing Christ.

I had thought that I might have been used by the church with regard to the children's movement here in UK but I had to be content with being Joel's wife and to realise that that was my priority of ministry before other things opened up.

We had no Sunday School in Plymouth, our first pastorate. Perhaps my ministry to children was finished? But I could not go to a prayer meeting without a burden coming on me to prayer for the children.

After two years we moved to Carmarthen where I was Sunday School superintendent.

'I don't know why I had eight children. I think some of them should have been yours,' Miriam teased. Well, at least they were mine to pray for.

Then we retired. No, it must have been re-tyred, for I found that my ministry was just beginning. The Lord had called me to write, and then the door opened for me to lecture on children's work in our Bible college, but what of the children in my own street? It was through my books, and I must say through prayer, that I had an opening into our local schools. Somehow I felt that all that had gone before had been to prepare me for this.

A child came up to me in the supermarket. 'You come to our school, don't you,' then turned to her mother and said, 'She tells us about Jesus.' Yes, they too are the children that God has given me.

(Oh yes, and with Joel's encouragement I did go on to get a degree.)

I have told my story. I have not done anything outstanding. It has not been more dynamic or adventuresome that any other, but I have told it because I trust it will show what God can do with someone who is very ordinary, someone that no one else would have chosen, and that it will show too that God is faithful and will never let us go.

Pauline and Joel

EPILOGUE

'Tell me, do you ever quarrel?' a courting couple had asked. 'Of course we do,' I responded, then added, 'but we make sure we make it up quickly. Life is too short.'

Joel was annoyed. 'Do we quarrel?' he challenged, when they had gone. I laughed. 'Oh, come on. Let's have a quarrel about whether or not we quarrel.'

If he were here I would not be able to write this. Well, maybe he did not quarrel, but I did not find marriage easy and could sometimes show annoyance. On one such occasion he gently asked, 'Tell me, do you love me?' I searched my heart. I had vowed in the presence of God to love him. Once I had admitted, 'Yes,' however grudgingly, the feelings of love flooded my heart. We were at one.

When we first married Joel found it very hard to express his love, and I had to declare my love without any apparent return, but gradually over the years he learned to put his love into words in the most delightful and unexpected ways.

When we first married Joel found it very hard to express affection, and I had to declare my love without any apparent return, but gradually over the years he learned to put his love into words in the most delightful and unexpected ways.

JOEL MY JO

I'm thanking God for you, Joel my Jo,
A gift from his heart, on that day long ago,
Delight to your parents, and Mama and Gi,
Who believed in God's promise of what you could be;-
For 'Jehovah is God' and Lord of your life,
And you heeded his call, and entered the strife.

Yes, J for Jehovah, and Jesus and joy,
And you trusted and proved him, though only a boy,
Until in the fullness of time you went forth,
Part of his body, a gift to his church;
None standing against you, and none need you fear,

Epilogue

God's word still your weapon as you face this new year.

But I'm thanking God for you, Joel my Jo,
That you came in my life, and together we go,
Looking ever to Jesus, who is always our joy
And we're facing the glory which none can destroy.
And though we still battle 'gainst Satan and sin,
Jehovah is God and in him we will win.

And today is your birthday, and with joy I now go
To thank the Lord for you, Joel my Jo.
(11th March, 1997)

Because Joel loved this little poem I wrote for his birthday I included it in my 'patchwork of Poetry,' and Joel told everyone, 'The last one is the best.' Joel's lovely niece, Anne, who has become a daughter to me, read it out at his funeral.

Yes, I had intended the previous chapter to be the last, a lovely 'happy ever after' ending to my story. Indeed, my book was advertised on the internet, the front cover showing a small plane flying over the mountains. But there was a hindrance. Somehow it could not be downloaded, and I believe God allowed this because he wanted another chapter written.

'Why a plane?' my artist friend, Bas, asked. 'The mission planes were significant in my life,' I replied. But then I realised, that had been just one chapter in my life. It is The Divine Eagle who has carried me on the wings of the morning.

Now he has come to stir up the sweet security of my nest with Joel and is teaching me to soar yet higher; always there to protect me when I feel I am plummeting to the depths. I am so privileged to have Bas's wonderful painting to bless those of you who take time to read my story.

'Do you think they are up there looking down on us?' my neighbour asked. Her father had died soon before Joel. The prophetic picture the Lord gave me so long ago, of walking together into the glory, came to mind. I was able to answer, 'I believe Joel is totally taken up with Jesus.'

156

We may not have walked together into the glory, but Joel is just a step ahead. He had a brief illness, a viral infection, they said. 'I'm sorry, he must go into hospital.' But God had something better. We came home to have some lunch before setting out, and his head fell onto my shoulder. He did not know pain, or old age. His was an abundant entrance into the Kingdom.

I'm painting rainbows as I write. It was many years ago the Lord told me, 'I am giving you a ministry of tears.' Now I am learning to thank God for the tears, yes, and the pain. It is because Joel was so special that my pain is so great, and God uses my tears not only for my healing but in some way to minister to others too, for there are many like myself. Jesus says, 'I have called you as a woman forsaken and grieved in spirit.' As my friend Sylvia tells me, 'It is a calling to be a widow.'

Peace and joy the Lord promised me when he spoke to me of taking the wings of the morning, and I still have to claim it, for it is our inheritance. And so I go on, my face 'Towards the Sunrise,' as I titled my book about the unnamed women of the Bible.

'The grief will always be there, but you must open your heart to all the little happinesses until your sky is filled with happiness.' I have many little happinesses and great big happinesses too. The love and care of family and friends, the joy of my ministry in the schools. I had heard about Walk through the Bible and since Joel's death God opened the way for me to train so that I am now a Bible Explorer, teaching this course as well as taking assemblies.

And there is 'Grace.' We came to retire in Porthcawl, believing God would use us to build up the small Apostolic fellowship there. In two years we saw growth and blessing and were getting known in the town. We were seeking a permanent building, but the powers that be decided that it must be closed, and all our resources go to the new work in Brackla. We were heart broken. But he was given a picture of a tree cut down to the stump and out of that stump a strong bough spreading along the ground.

Doors began to open for us to minister in the many chapels around. Was the this the bough spreading? Then God spoke clearly to us of again opening an apostolic work. We were full of faith and joy, though we didn't know how God would work.

'I believe the Lord is going to do great things.' These were almost Joel's last words.

Epilogue

God is doing great things. Brackla are planting 'Grace Community church' in Porthcawl, and I know that I have come to the kingdom 'for such a time as this.'

Who knows what the future holds? Maybe there are more chapters to be written, but they will have to be in another book, for it is time, once more, to close. I have been blessed in writing, and I pray in some small way you have been blessed in reading.

Wings of the Morning

Epilogue

Printed in the United Kingdom
by Lightning Source UK Ltd.
109225UKS00001B/94-294